TEACH YOURSELF TO PLAY
GUITAR
Acoustic Guitar Songbook

ISBN 1-4234-1023-8

HAL•LEONARD®
CORPORATION
7777 W. BLUEMOUND RD. P.O. BOX 13819 MILWAUKEE, WI 53213

T0057634

Visit Hal Leonard Online at
www.halleonard.com

About a Girl

Words and Music by Kurt Cobain

Tune down 1/2 step:
(low to high) E♭-A♭-D♭-G♭-B♭-E♭

Chorus

have a ___ clue. ___   I'll take ad - van - tage   while ___

you hang me ___ out to dry, ___   but I can't see you   ev -'ry   night ___   (1., 2. for)

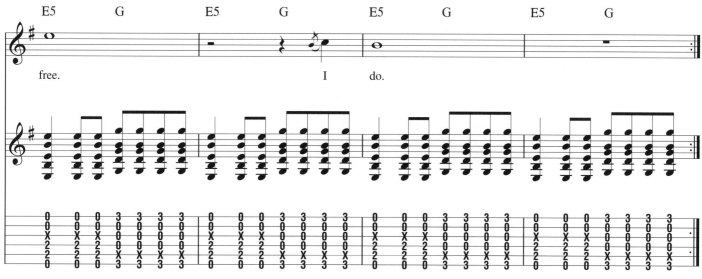

free.   I   do.

Guitar Solo

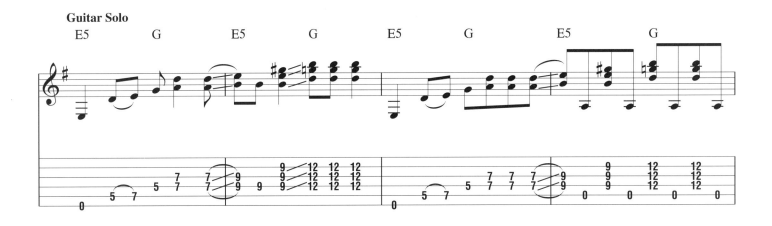

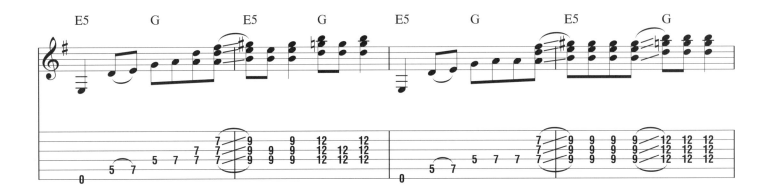

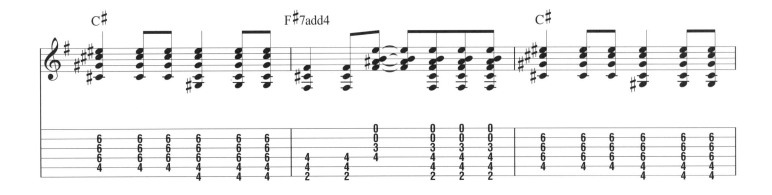

D.C. al Coda
(no repeats)

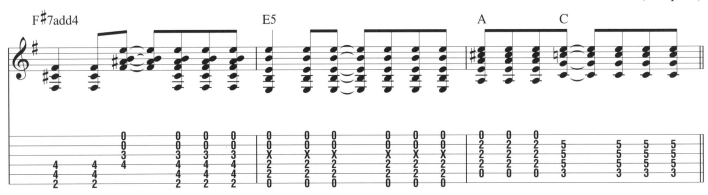

Coda

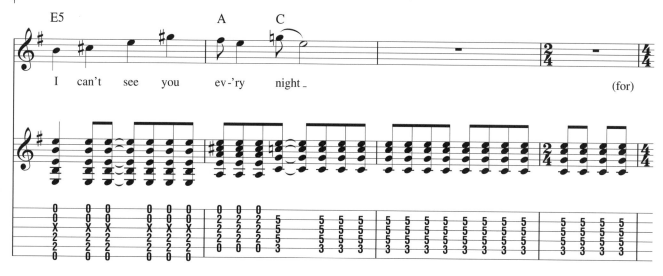

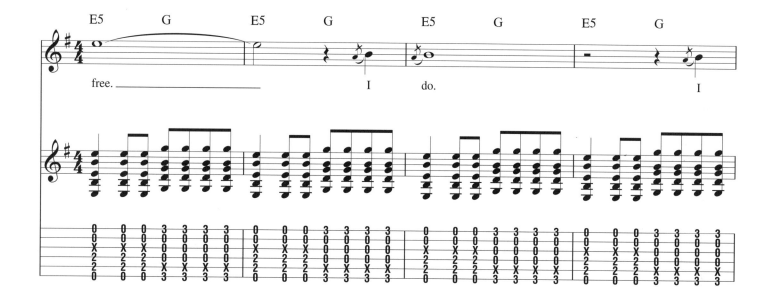

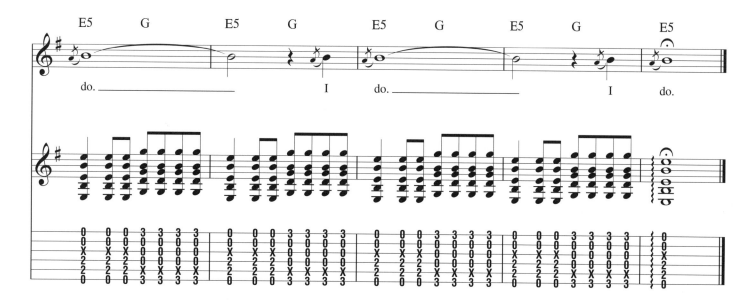

Additional Lyrics

2. I'm standing in your line,
   I do, hope you have the time.
   I do, pick a number to,
   I do, keep a date with you.

Babe, I'm Gonna Leave You

Words and Music by Anne Bredon, Jimmy Page and Robert Plant

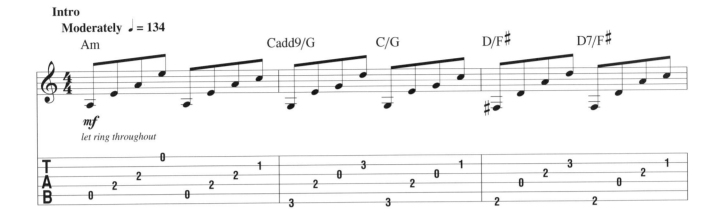

ba - by, ba - by, I'm___ gon - na leave___ you.___

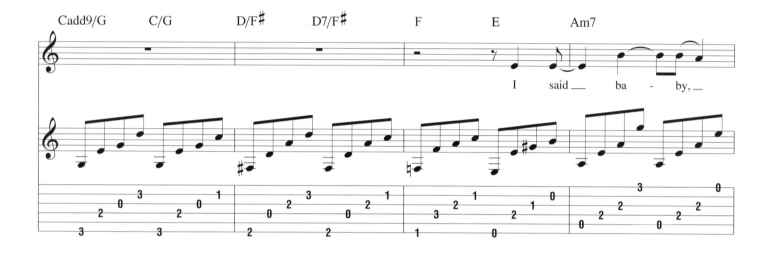

I said ___ ba - by, ___

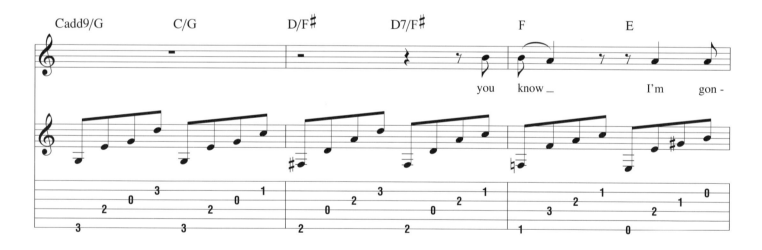

you know ___ I'm gon -

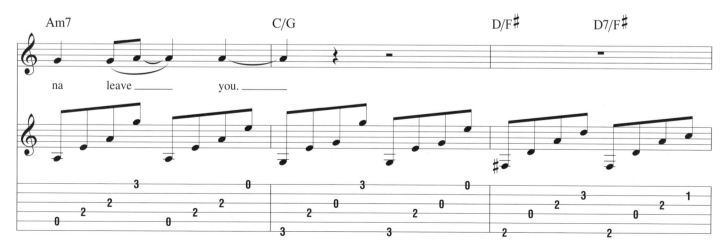

na leave _____ you. _____

I'll _____ leave you ____ when ___ the sum - mer - time, _____

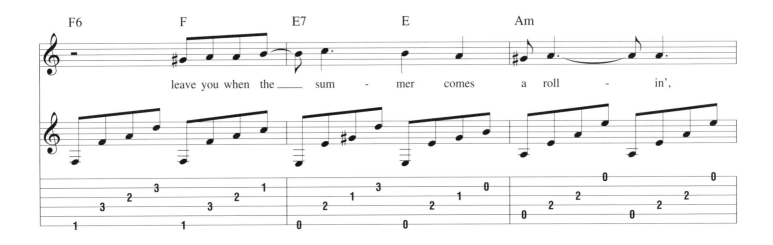

leave you when the _____ sum - mer comes a roll - in',

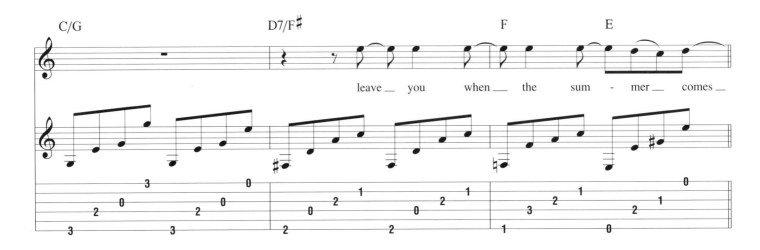

leave ___ you ___ when ___ the sum - mer ___ comes ___

Interlude

Play 3 times

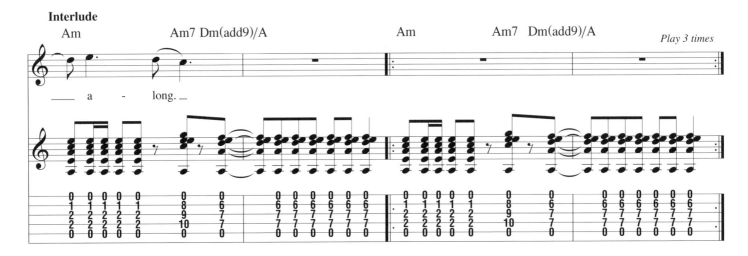

___ a - long. ___

Verse

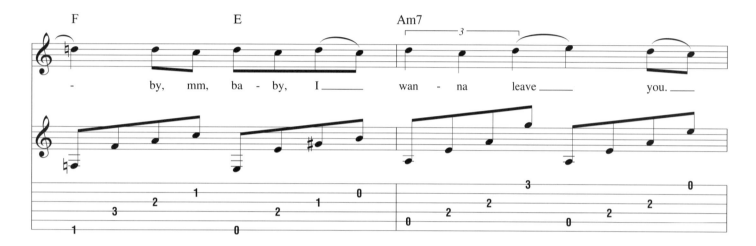

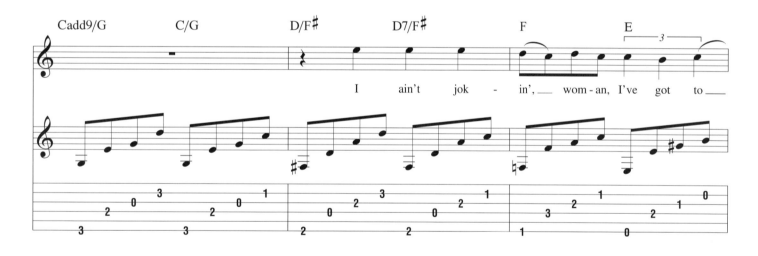

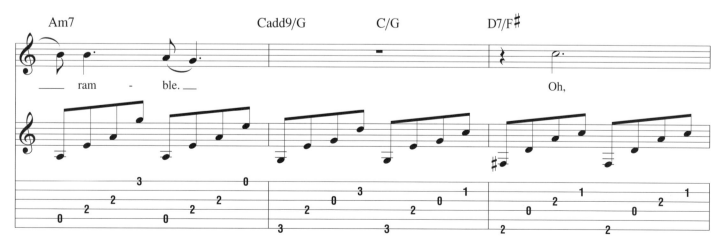

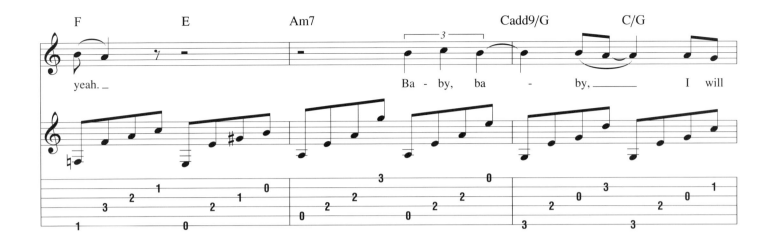

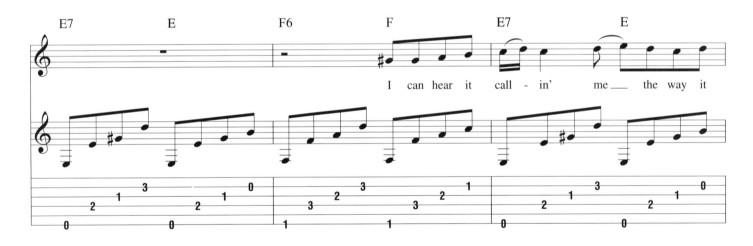

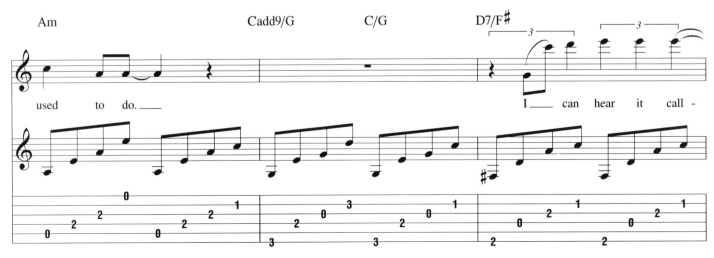

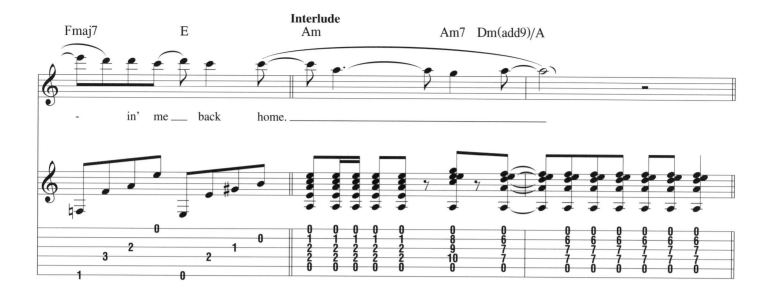

-in' me ___ back home. ___

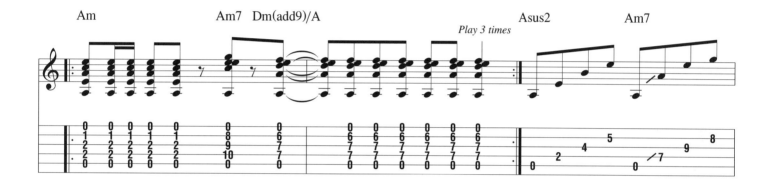

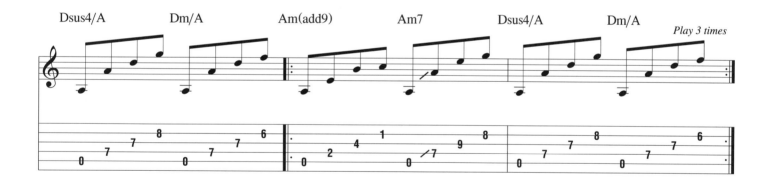

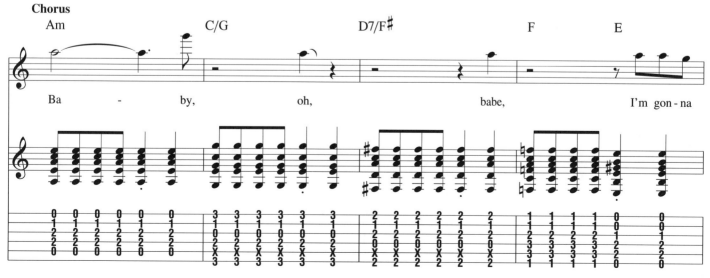

Ba - by, oh, babe, I'm gon - na

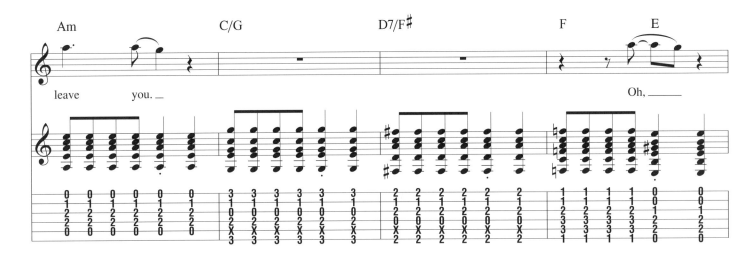

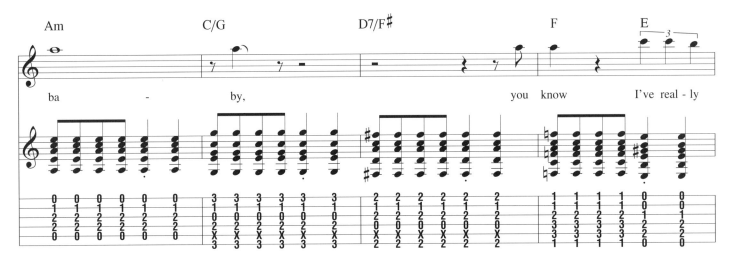

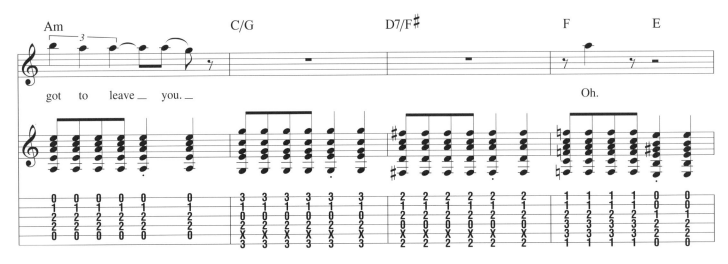

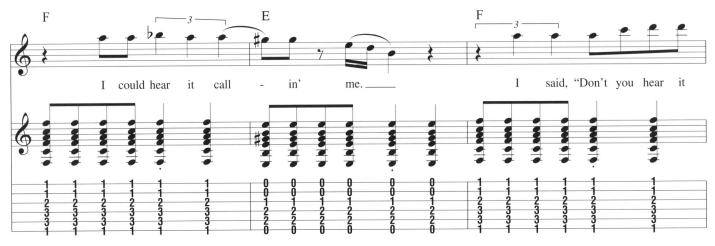

Interlude

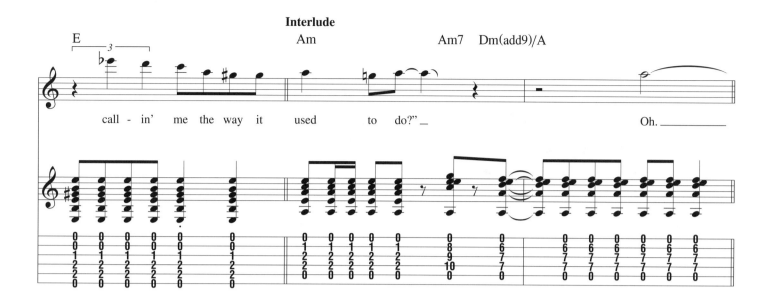

call - in' me the way it used to do?" _ Oh. _____

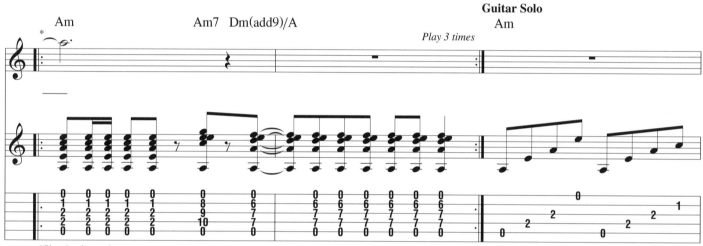

*Sing 1st time only.

Guitar Solo

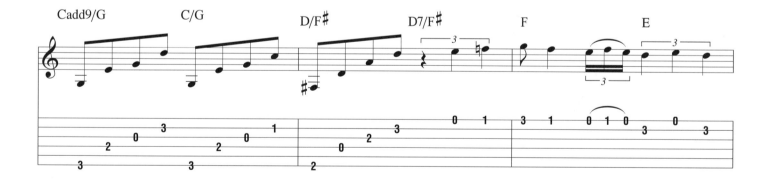

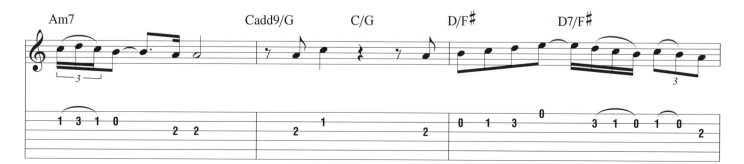

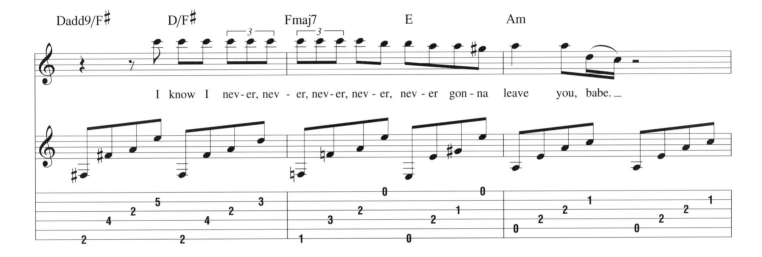

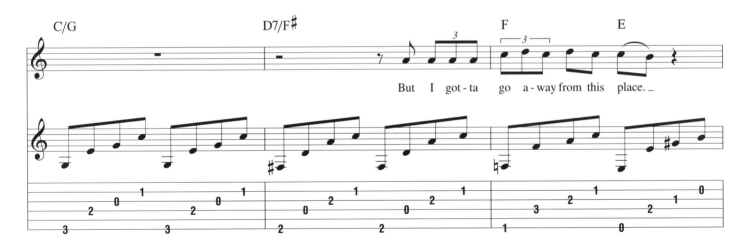

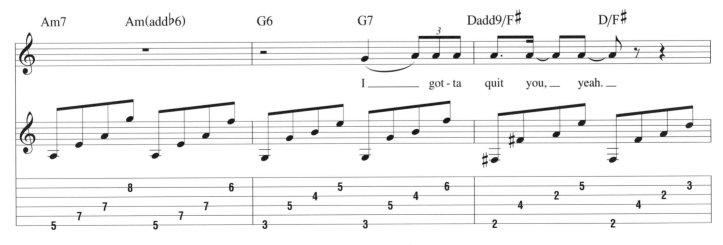

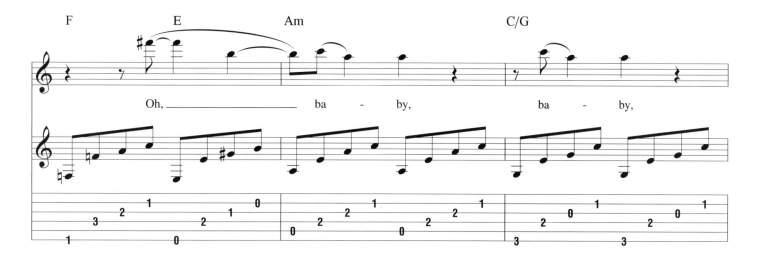

Oh, ____ ba - by, ba - by,

ba - by, ____ ba - by. ____ **Interlude** Ba - by, ____

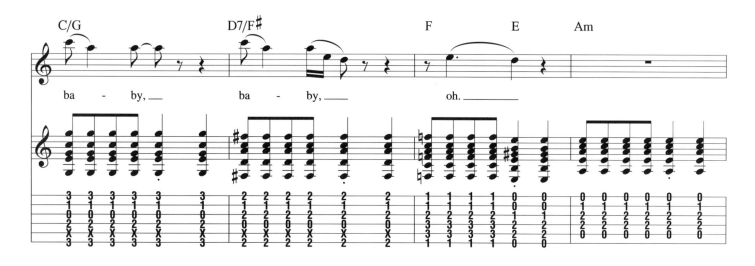

ba - by, ____ ba - by, ____ oh. ____

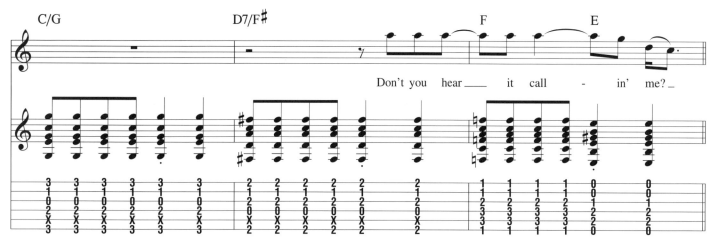

Don't you hear ____ it call - in' me? ____

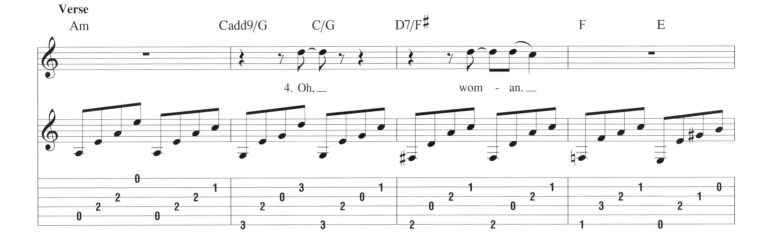

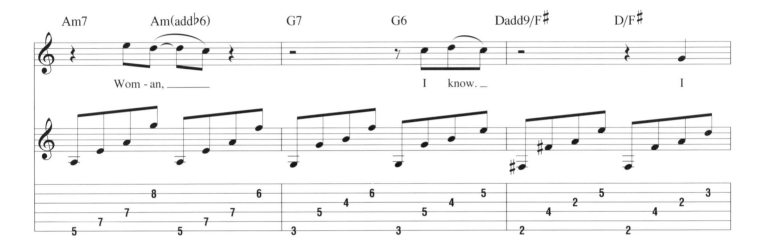

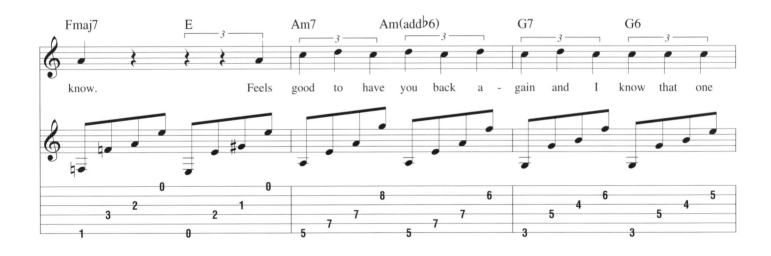

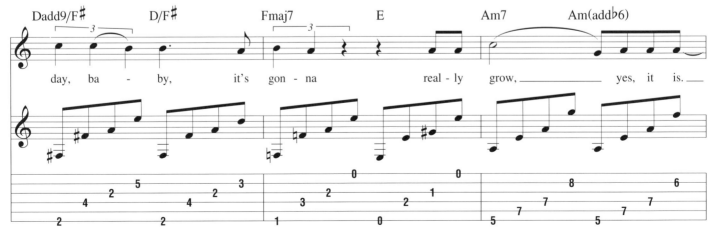

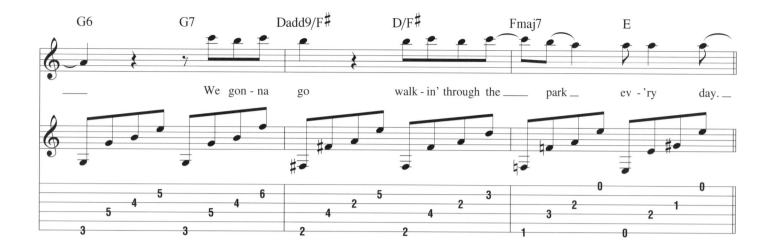

Interlude

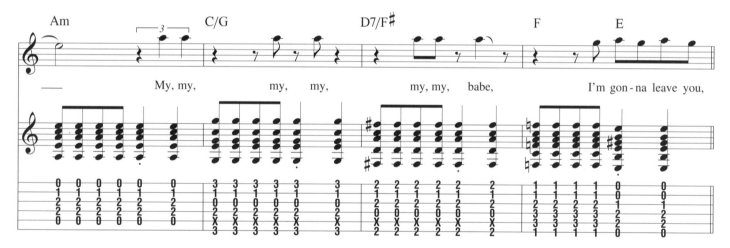

Guitar Solo

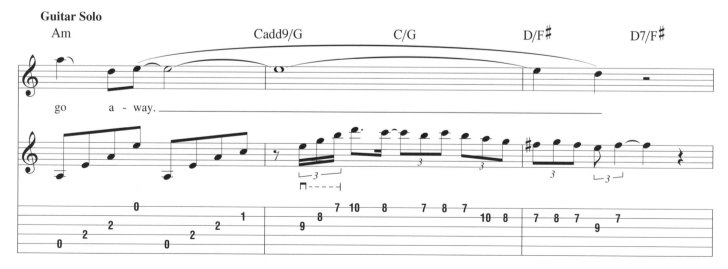

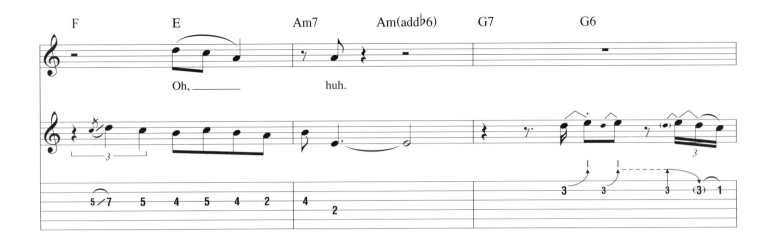

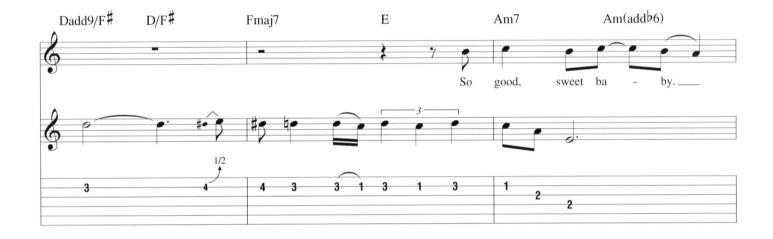

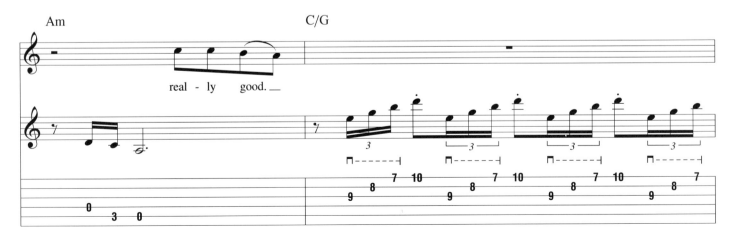

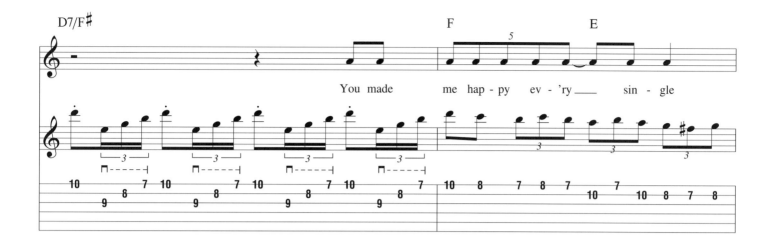

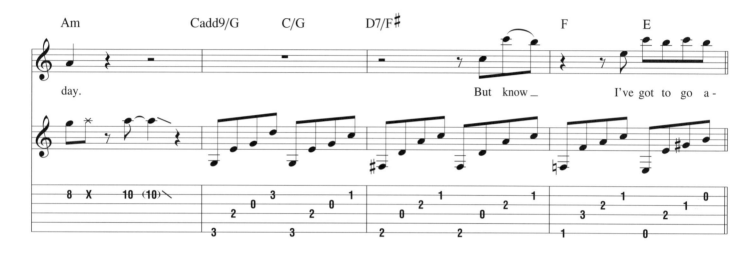

Interlude

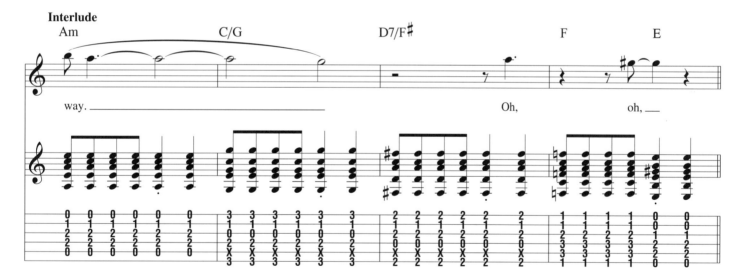

w/ Voc. ad lib. on repeats

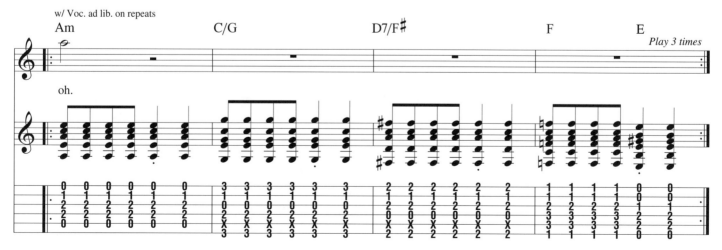

Outro
Free time

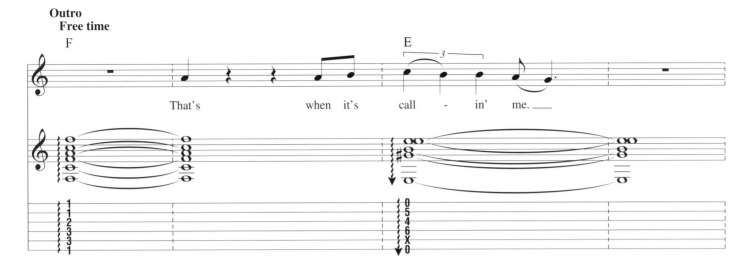

Lyrics: That's when it's call - in' me. ____

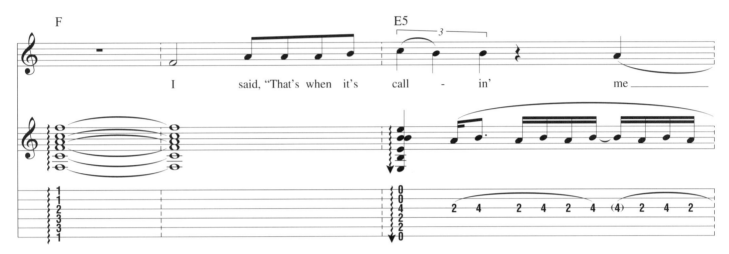

Lyrics: I said, "That's when it's call - in' me _____

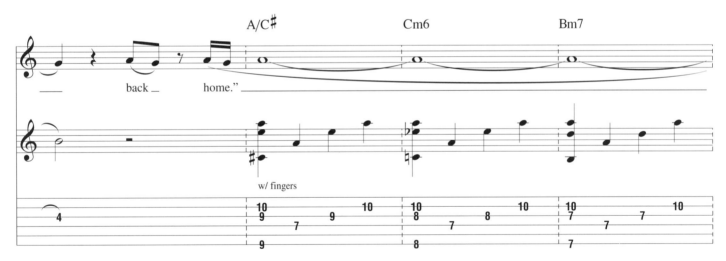

Lyrics: ____ back ____ home." _____

w/ fingers

Every Rose Has Its Thorn

Words and Music by Bobby Dall, Brett Michaels, Bruce Johannesson and Rikki Rocket

Tune down 1/2 step:
(low to high) E♭-A♭-D♭-G♭-B♭-E♭

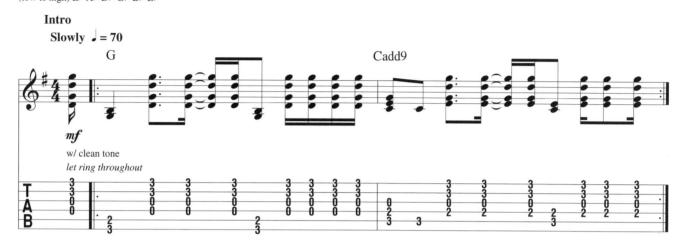

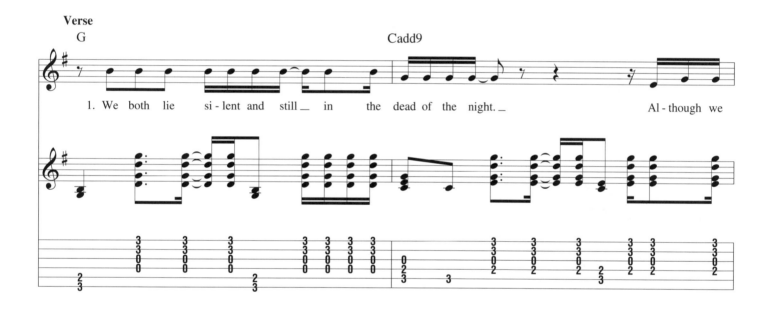

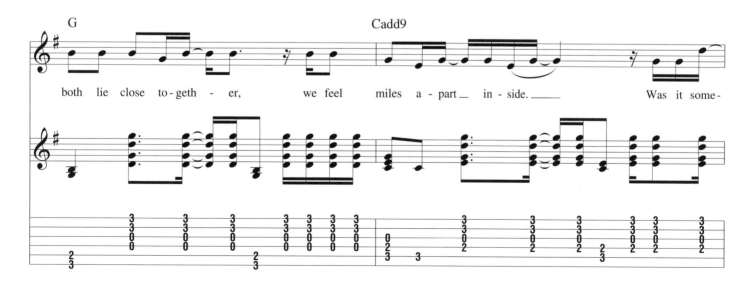

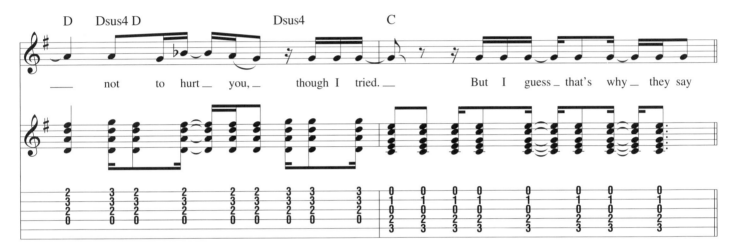

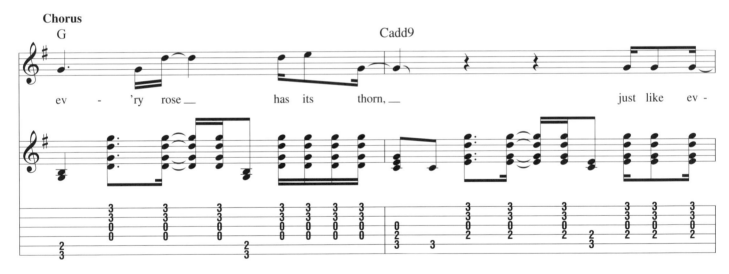

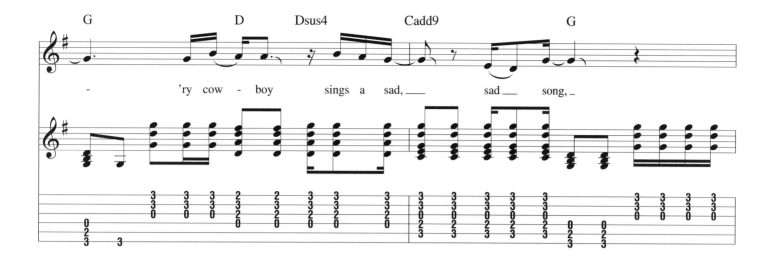

'ry cow - boy   sings a sad,___   sad___ song,___

ev - 'ry   rose ___   has   its   thorn. _____   Yeah, it   does. ___

w/ dist.

Interlude

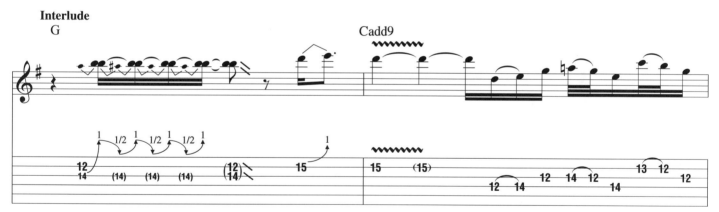

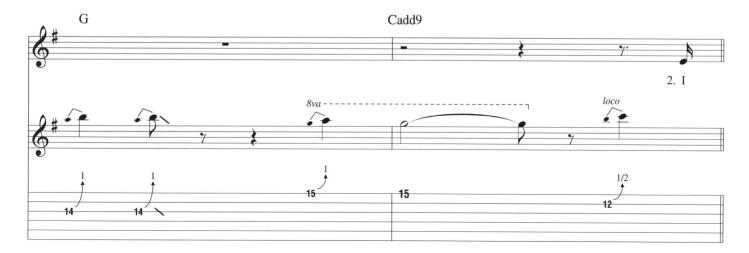

2. I

Verse

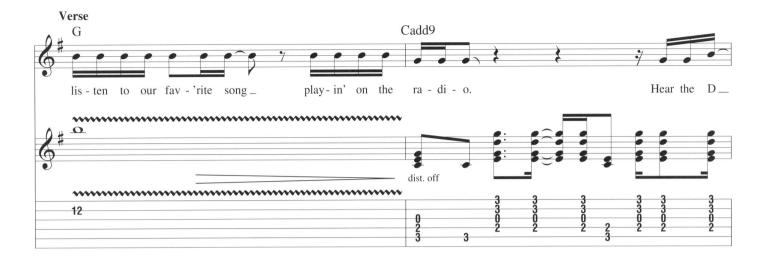

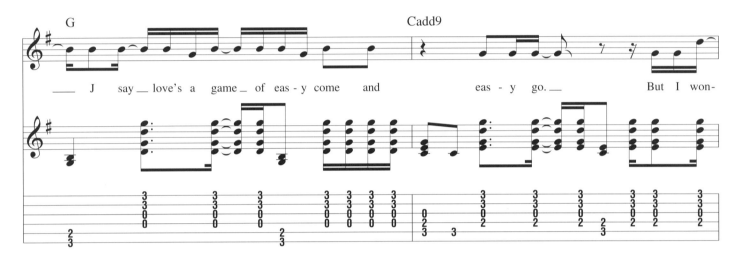

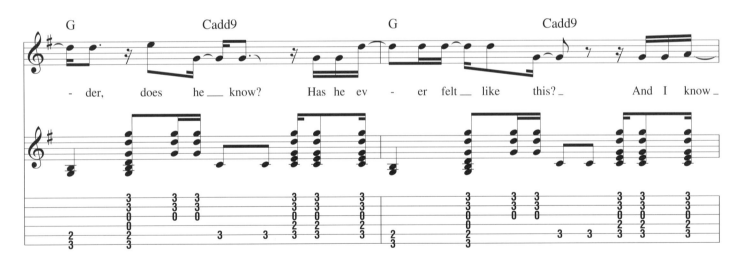

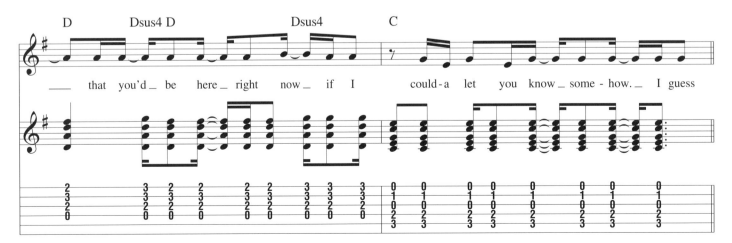

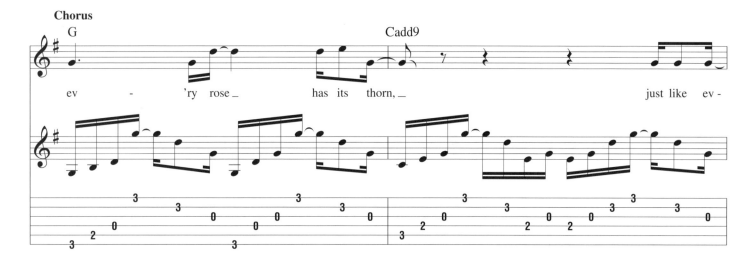

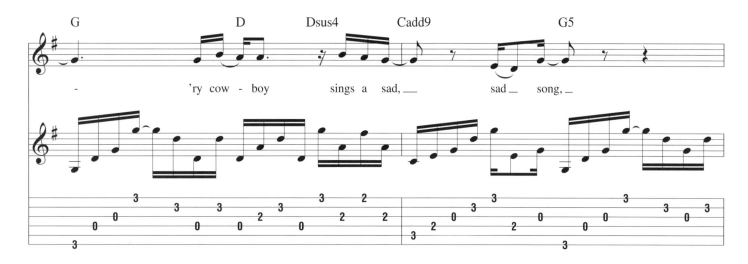

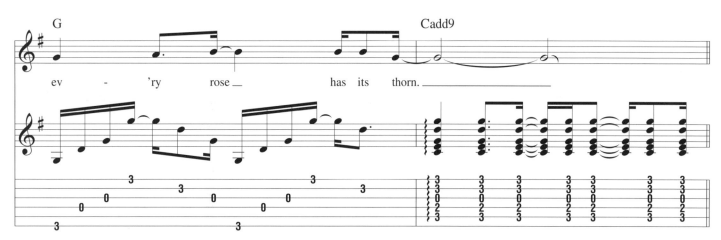

Bridge

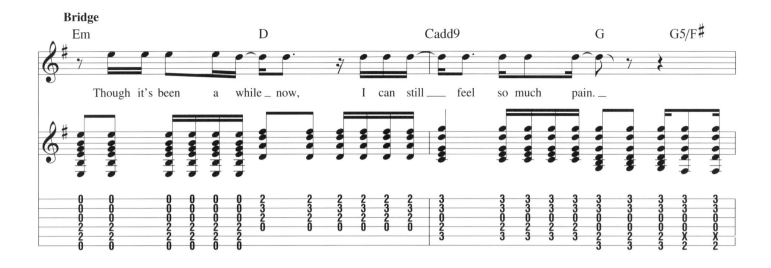

Though it's been a while now, I can still feel so much pain.

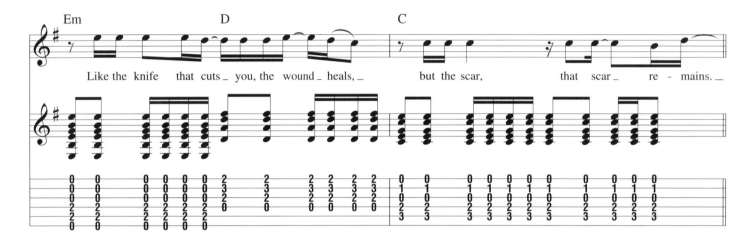

Like the knife that cuts you, the wound heals, but the scar, that scar remains.

Guitar Solo

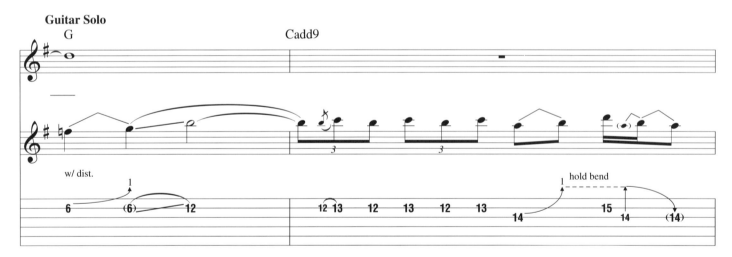

w/ dist.

hold bend

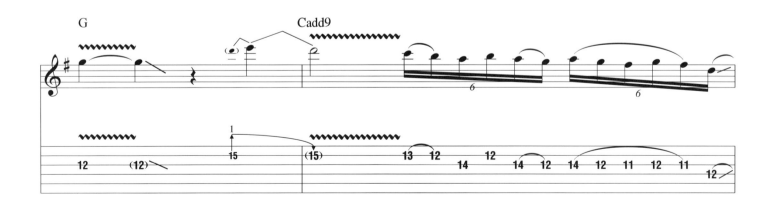

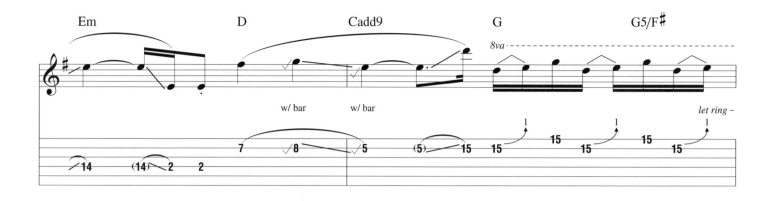

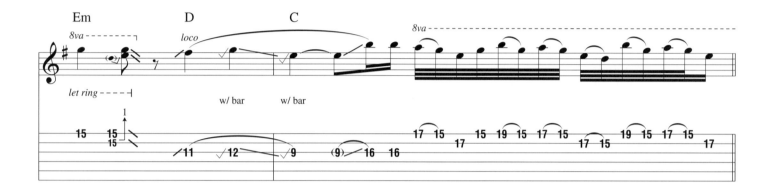

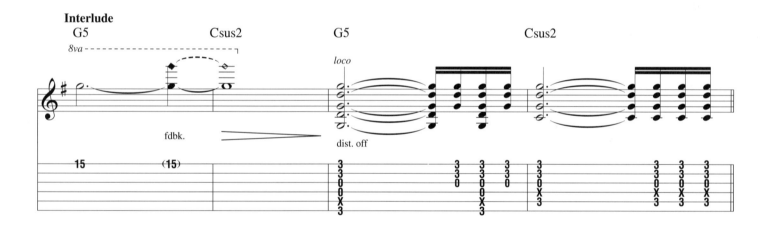

3. I know I could-a saved a love that night _ if I'd known what to say. _

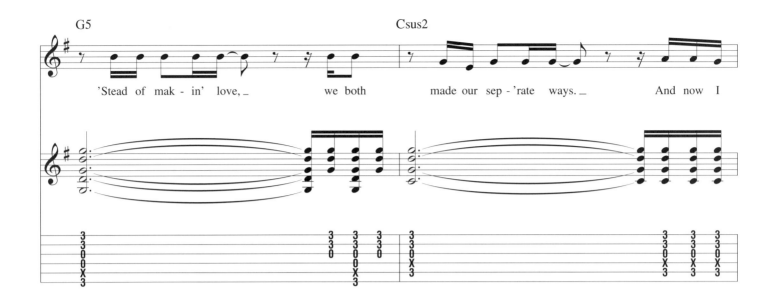

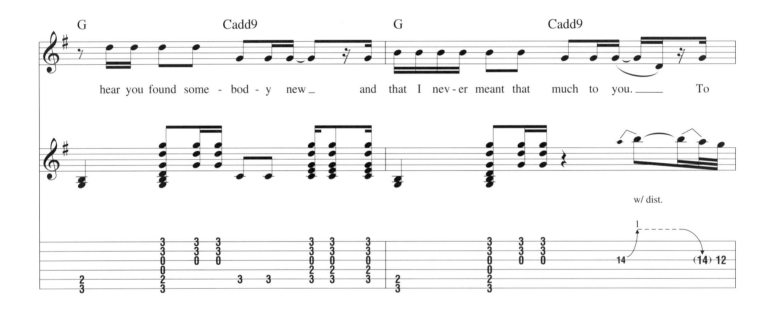

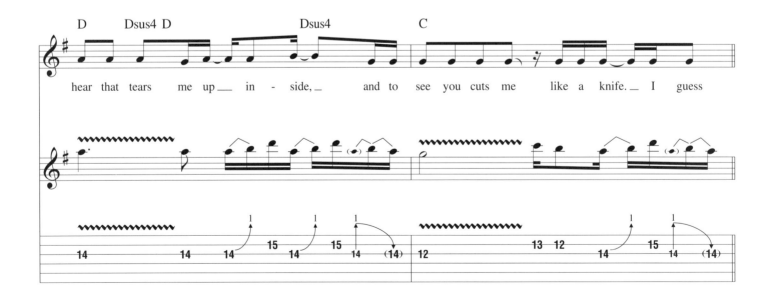

Chorus

ev - 'ry rose ___ has its thorn, ___   just like ev -

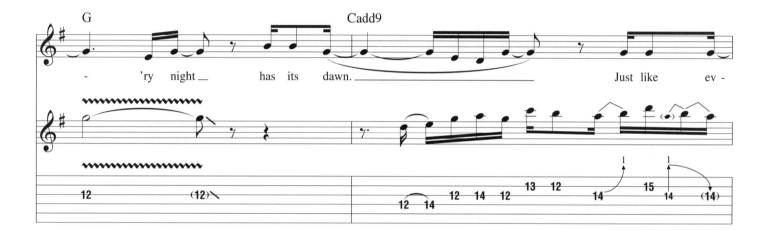

- 'ry night ___ has its dawn. _____   Just like ev -

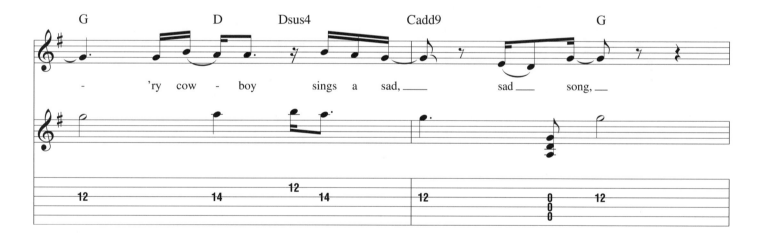

- 'ry cow - boy   sings a sad, ___   sad ___ song, ___

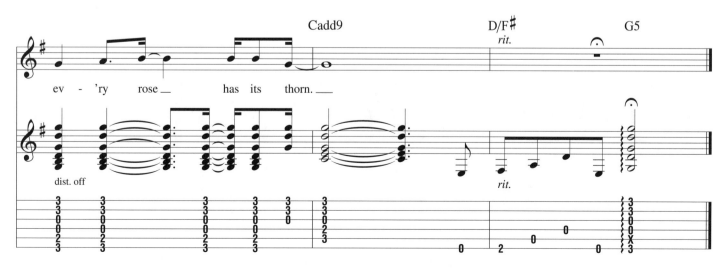

ev - 'ry rose ___ has its thorn. ___

Best of My Love

Words and Music by John David Souther, Don Henley and Glenn Frey

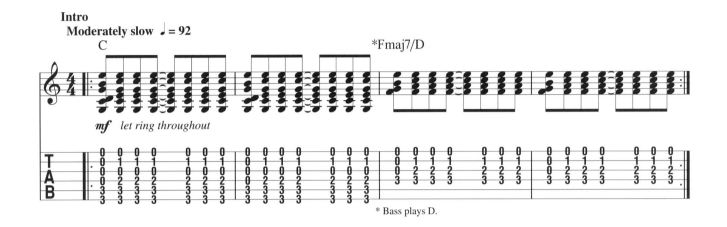

* Bass plays D.

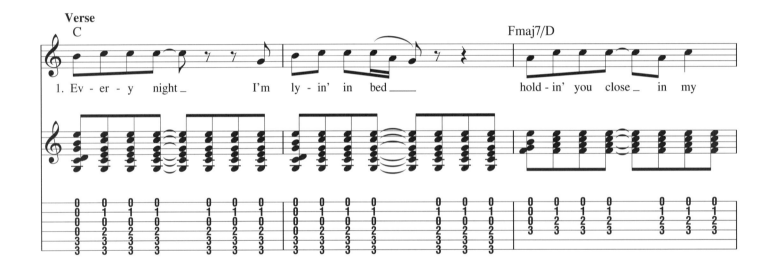

1. Ev-er-y night _ I'm ly-in' in bed _ hold-in' you close _ in my

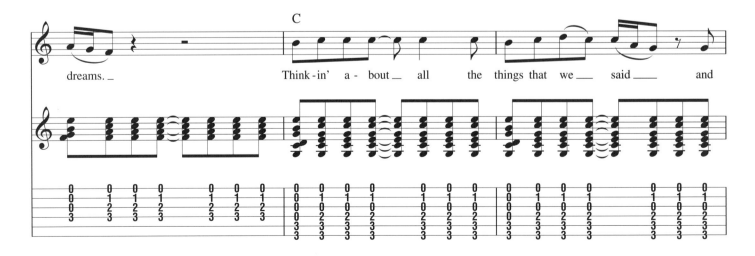

dreams. _ Think-in' a-bout _ all the things that we _ said _ and

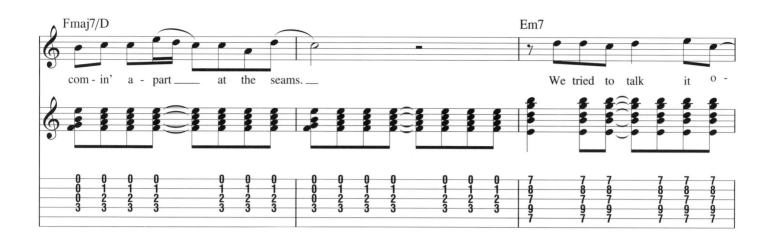

com - in' a - part ___ at the seams. ___ We tried to talk it o -

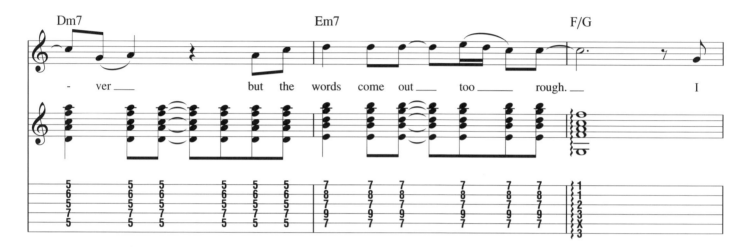

- ver ___ but the words come out ___ too ___ rough. ___ I

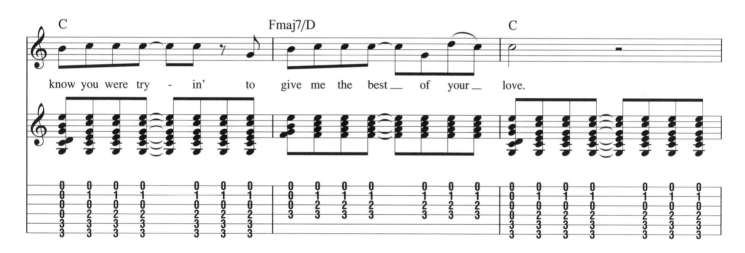

know you were try - in' to give me the best ___ of your ___ love.

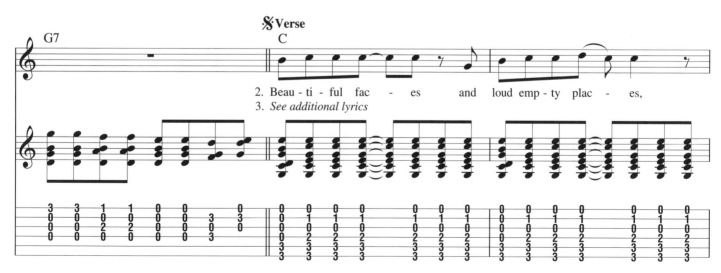

𝄋 **Verse**

2. Beau - ti - ful fac - es and loud emp - ty plac - es,
3. *See additional lyrics*

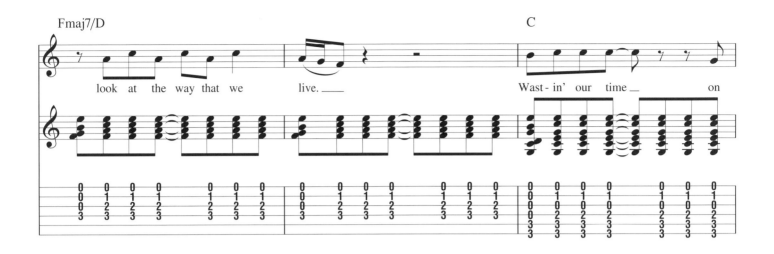

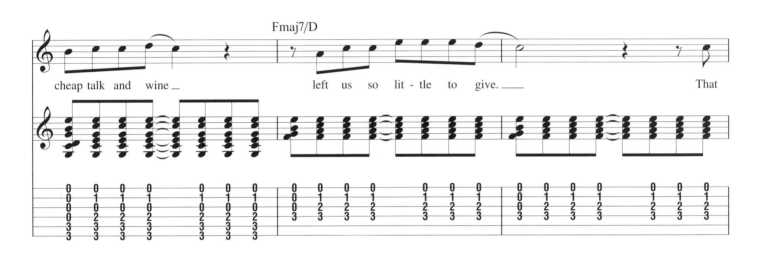

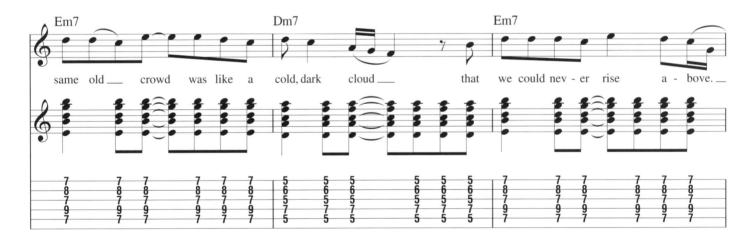

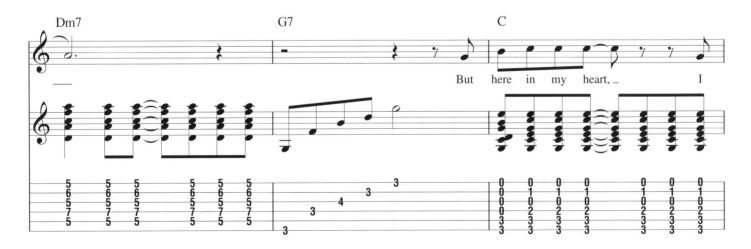

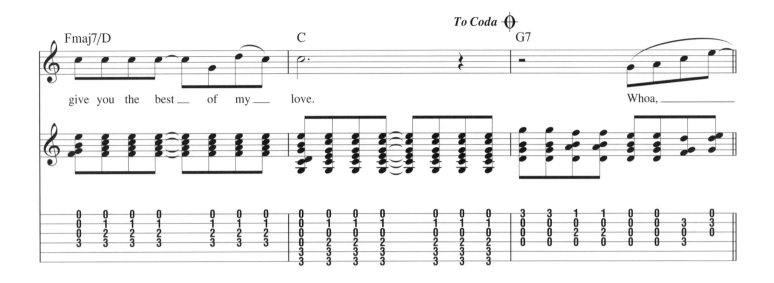

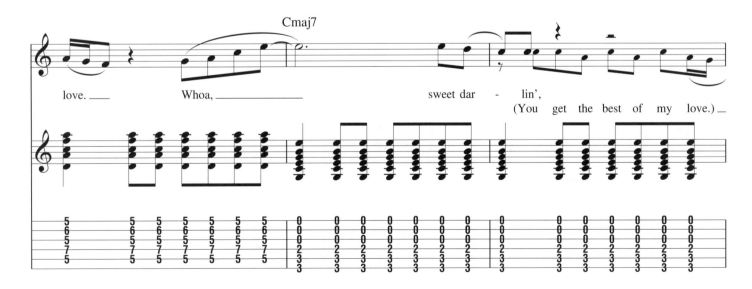

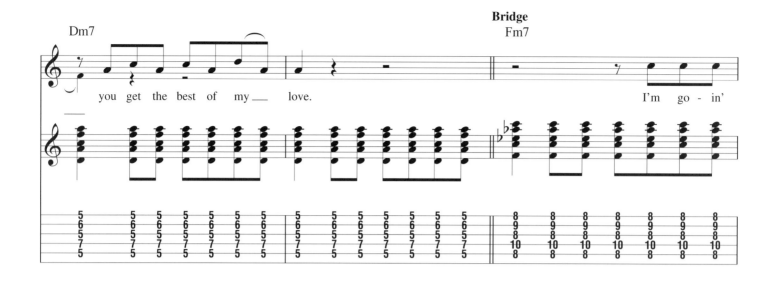

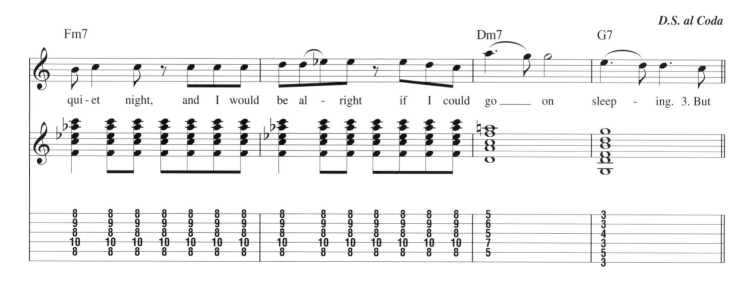

Coda

Outro-Chorus

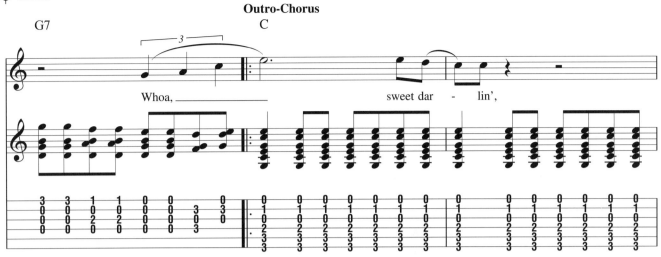

Whoa, _____ sweet dar - lin',

you get the best of my love. ____ Whoa, _____ sweet dar -

Repeat and fade

- lin,' you get the best of my ___ love. Whoa, _____

Additional Lyrics

3. But ev'ry morning I wake up and worry
   What's gonna happen today.
   You see it your way and I'll see it mine,
   But we both see it slippin' away.
   You know we always had each other, baby.
   I guess that wasn't enough.
   Oh, oh, but here in my heart,
   I give you the best of my love.

Night Moves

Words and Music by Bob Seger

Capo I

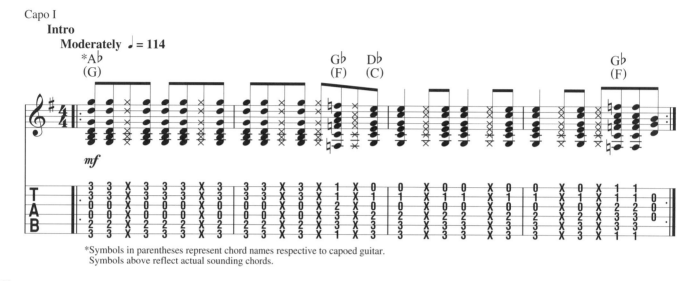

*Symbols in parentheses represent chord names respective to capoed guitar.
Symbols above reflect actual sounding chords.

Verse

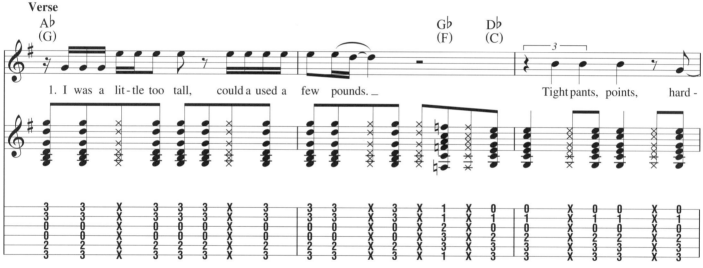

1. I was a lit-tle too tall, could a used a few pounds. ___ Tight pants, points, hard-

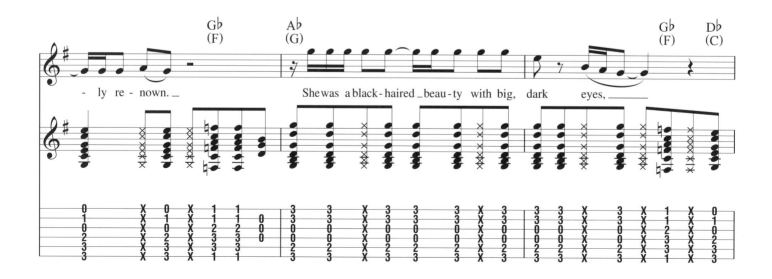

-ly re-nown. ___ She was a black-haired beau-ty with big, dark eyes, _____

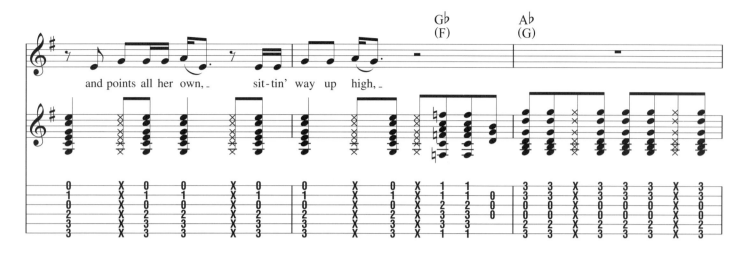

and points all her own, __ sit-tin' way up high, __

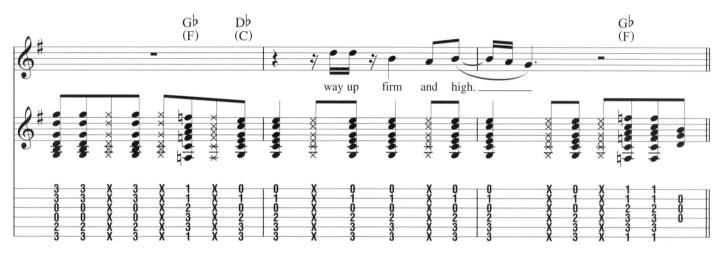

way up firm and high. _____

Verse

2. Out past the corn - fields, where the woods __ got heav - y,

out in the back seat of my six -

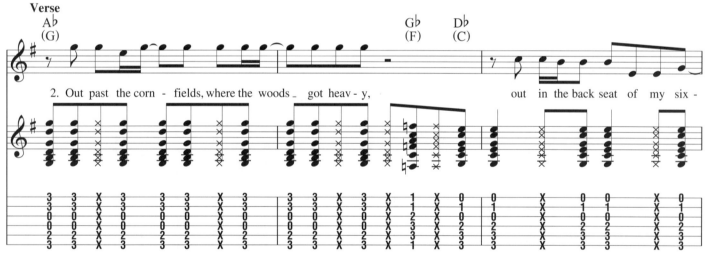

- ty Chev - y,

work - ing __ on mys-t'ries with - out __ an - y clues. _____

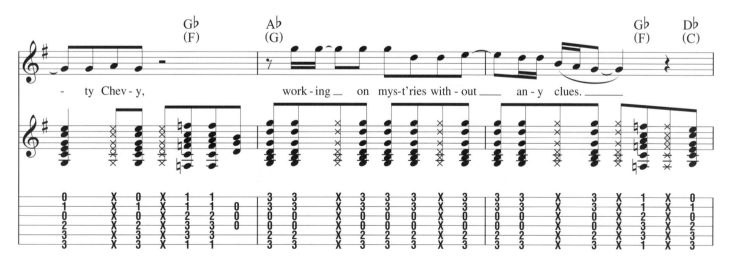

%: **Chorus**

Work-in' on our night moves, ___ try'n' to make _ some

See additional lyrics

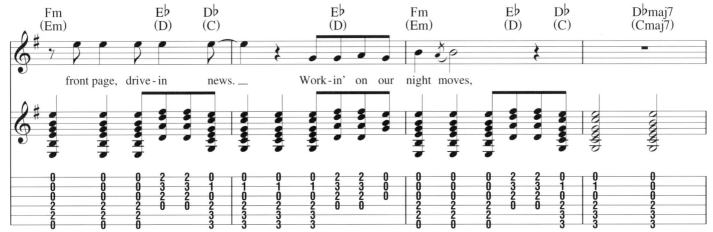

front page, drive-in news. __ Work-in' on our night moves,

in the sum-mer-time. ___ Mm, ___

To Coda ⊕

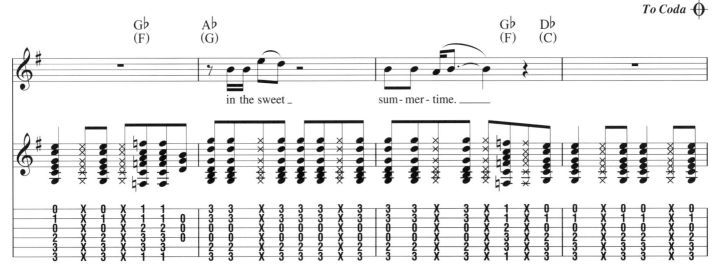

in the sweet _ sum-mer-time. ___

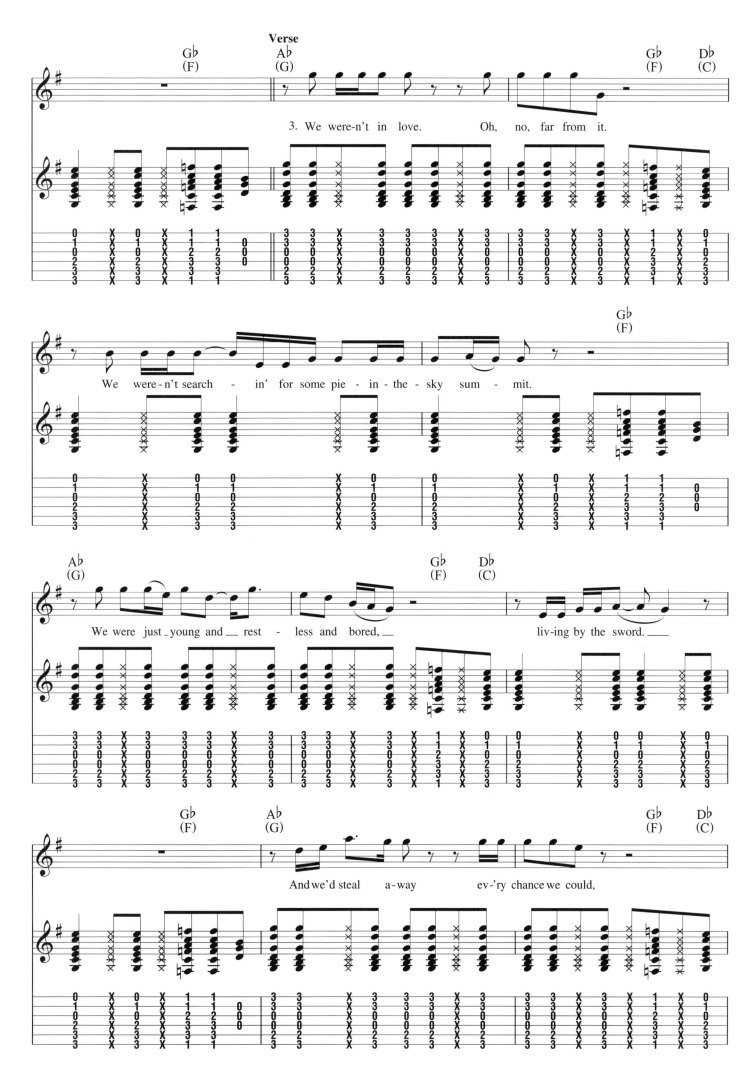

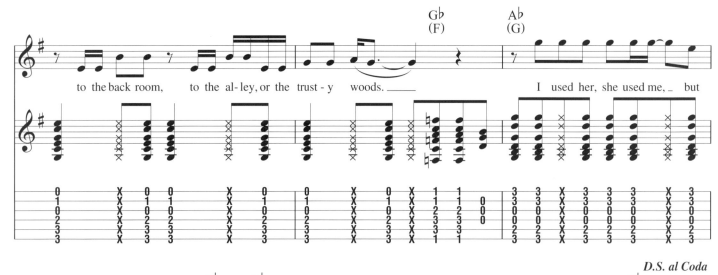

to the back room, to the al-ley, or the trust-y woods. _____ I used her, she used me, _ but

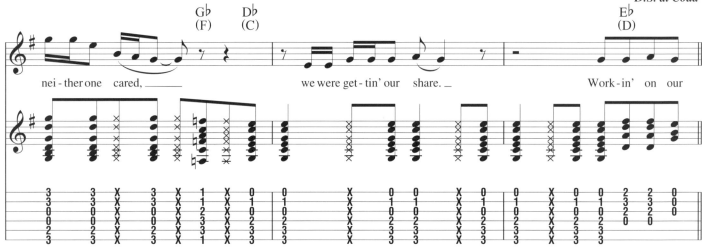

D.S. al Coda

nei-ther one cared, _____ we were get-tin' our share. _ Work-in' on our

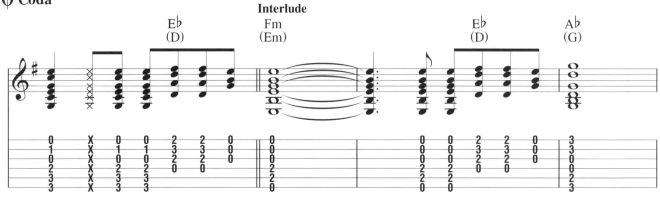

Coda

Interlude

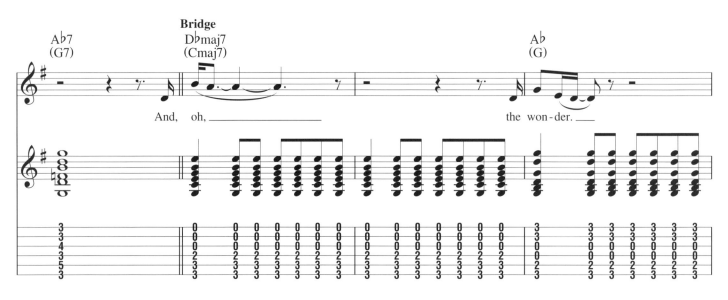

And, oh, _____ the won-der. _____

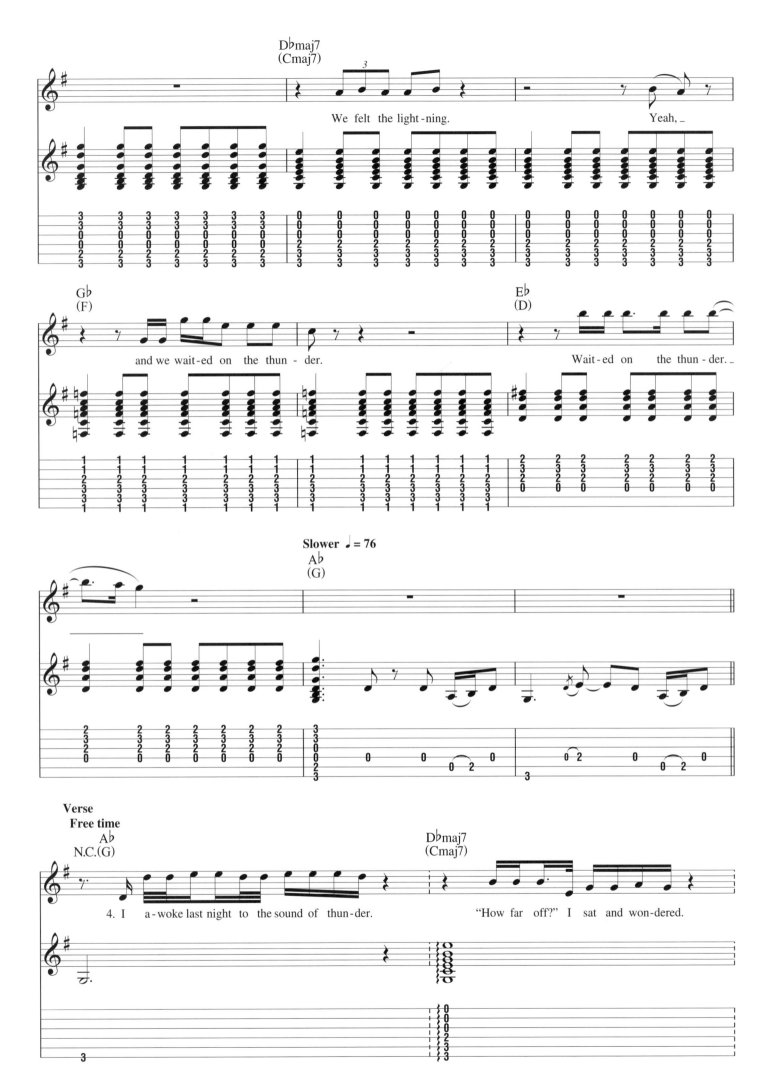

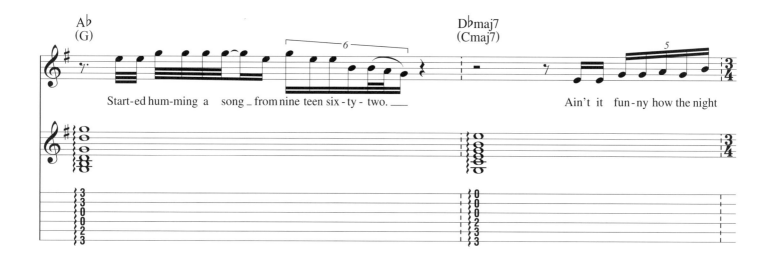

Start-ed hum-ming a song _ from nine teen six-ty - two. _ Ain't it fun-ny how the night

moves? _ When you just don't seem to have as much to lose. _____

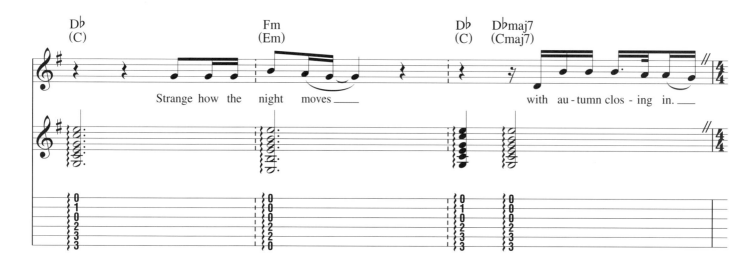

Strange how the night moves _____ with au-tumn clos-ing in. _

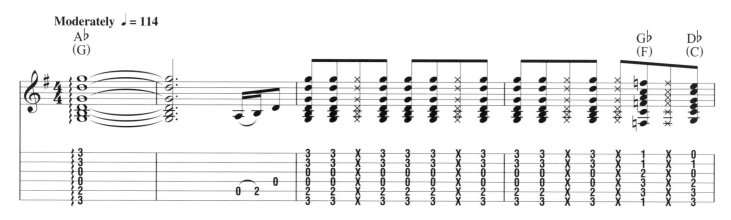

Moderately ♩ = 114

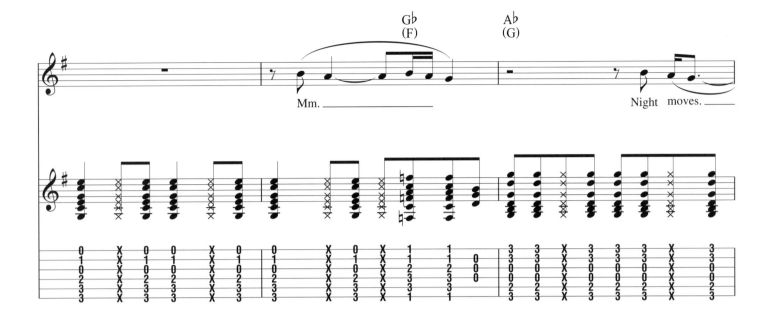

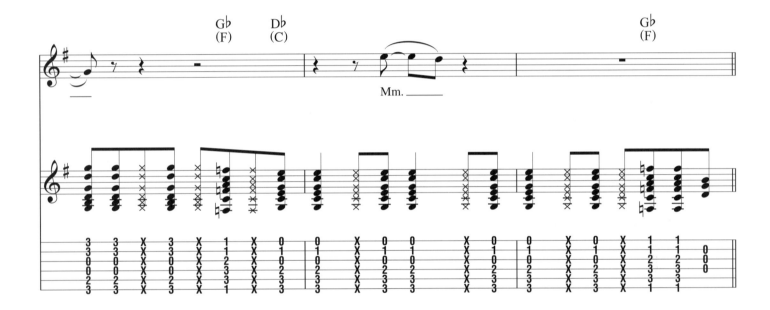

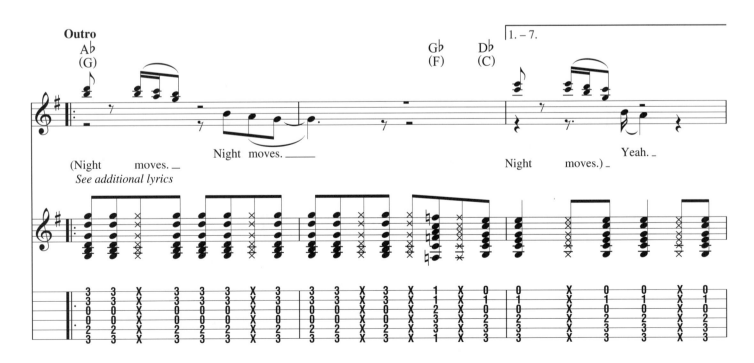

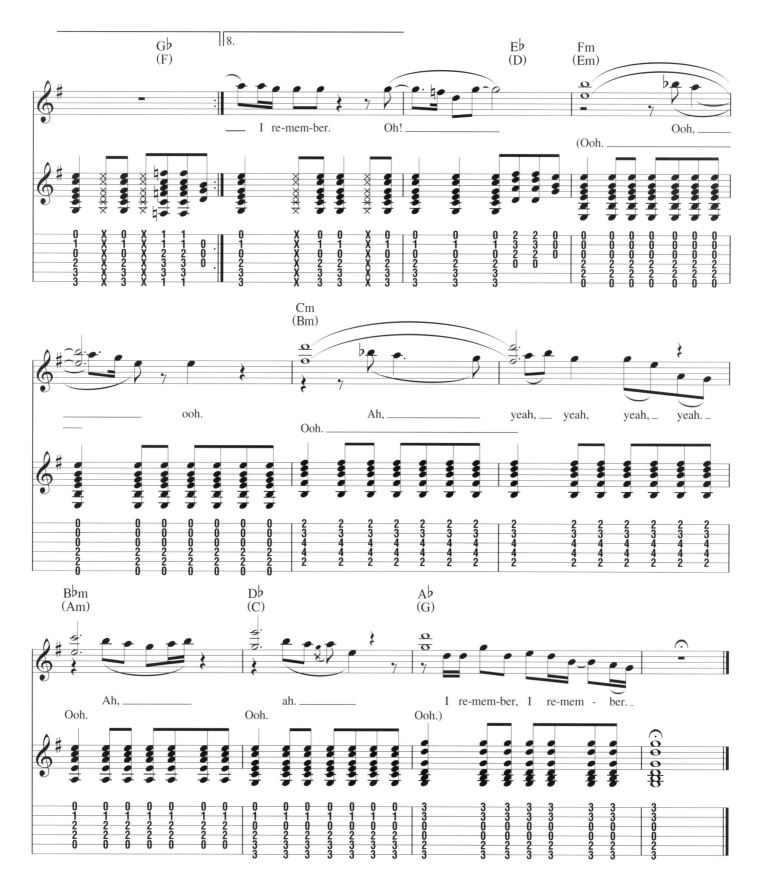

Additional Lyrics

Chorus Workin' on our night moves,
Tryin' to lose the awkward teenage blues.
Workin' on our night moves, mm,
And it was summertime, mm,
Sweet summertime, summertime.

Outro Moves, I sure remember the night moves.
In the morning, I remember.
Funny how you remember.
I remember, I remember, I remember, I remember.
Oh, oh, oh.
Keep it workin', workin' and practicin'.
Workin' and practicin' all of the night moves.
Night moves. Oh.
I remember, yeah, yeah, yeah, I remember.
Ooh. I remember, Lord, I remember, Lord, I remember.

Signs

Words and Music by Les Emmerson

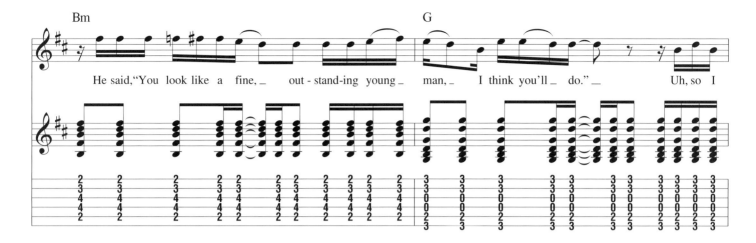

He said, "You look like a fine, _ out-stand-ing young _ man, _ I think you'll _ do." _ Uh, so I

took off my hat and said, "I-mag-ine that, huh, me a work-ing for you." _ Oh. _____

Chorus

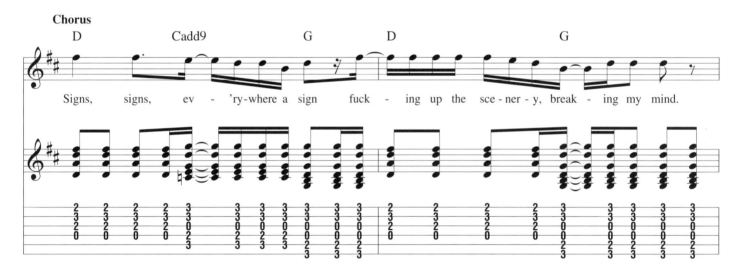

Signs, signs, ev-'ry-where a sign fuck - ing up the sce-ner-y, break-ing my mind.

1.

To Coda ⊕

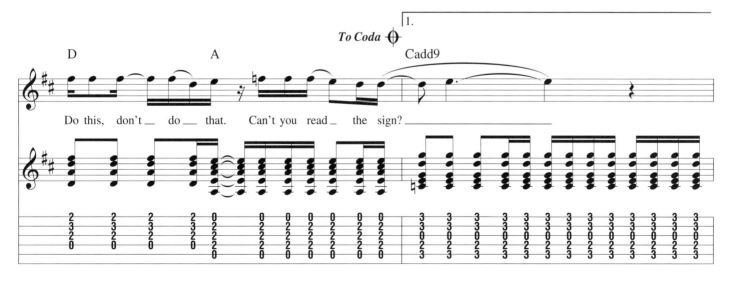

Do this, don't _ do _ that. Can't you read _ the sign? _____

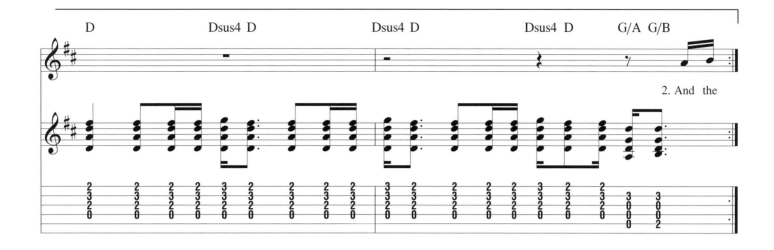

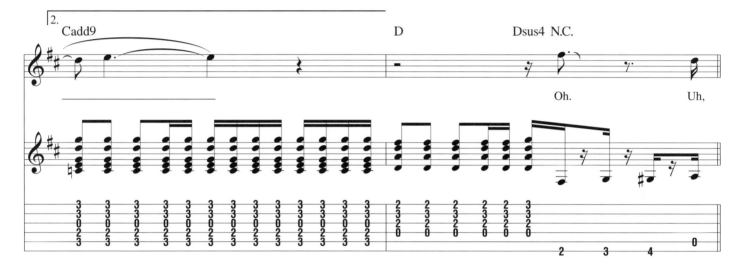

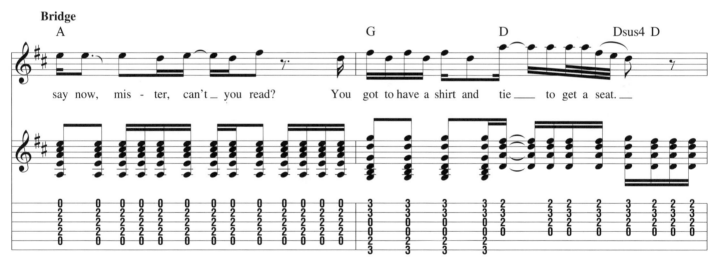

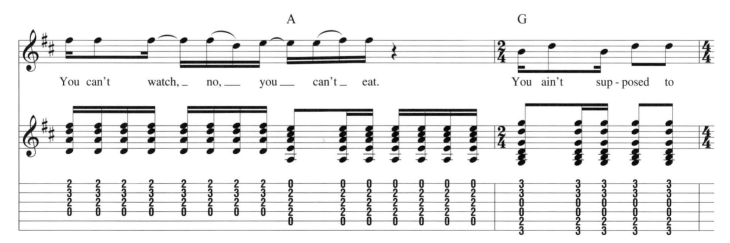

be here. _____ And the

sign said, "You got to have a mem-ber-ship card to get in-side." _ Ooh!

Guitar Solo

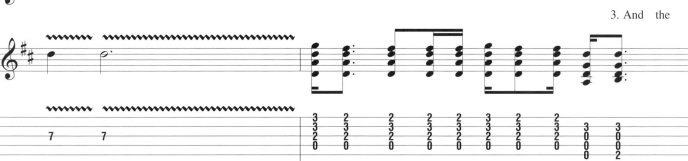

3. And the

⊕ **Coda**

Outro

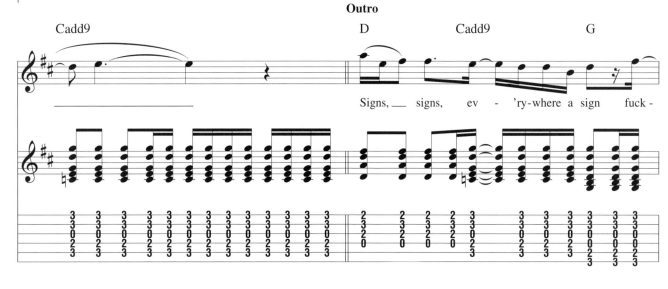

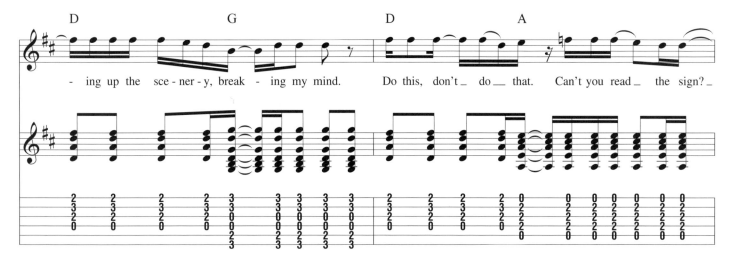

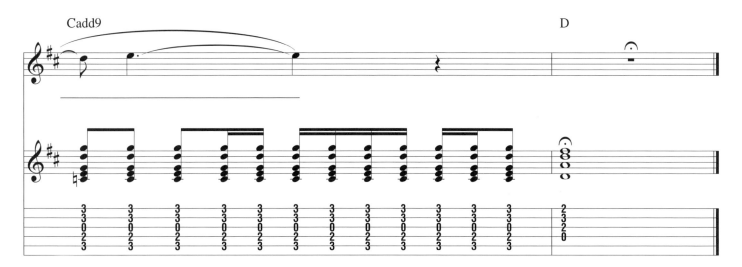

Additional Lyrics

2. And the sign says, "Anybody caught trespassing will be shot on sight."
   So I jumped the fence and yelled at the house, "Hey, what gives you the right
   To put up a fence to keep me out or to keep Mother Nature in?"
   If God was here he'd tell it to your face, "Man, you're some kinda sinner."

3. And the sign says, "Everybody welcome, come in and kneel down and pray."
   And then they pass around the plate at the end of it all, and I didn't have a penny to pay.
   So I got me a pen and paper, and I made up my own fuckin' sign.
   I said, "Thank you, Lord, for thinkin' about me, I'm alive and doing fine."

Norwegian Wood (This Bird Has Flown)

Words and Music by John Lennon and Paul McCartney

Capo II

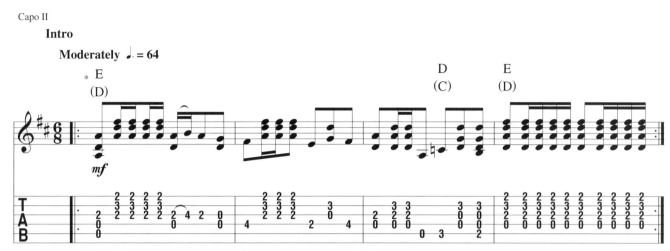

*Symbols in parentheses represent chord names respective to capoed guitar.
Symbols above reflect actual sounding chords. Capoed fret is "0" in tab.

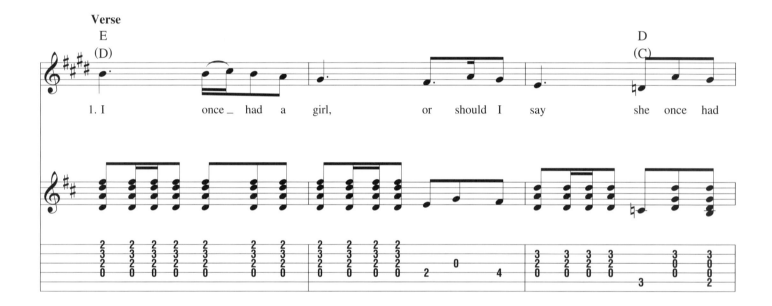

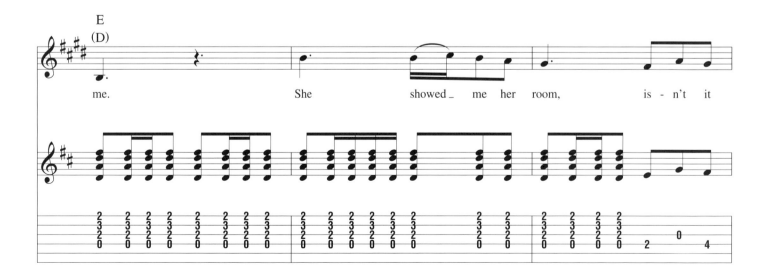

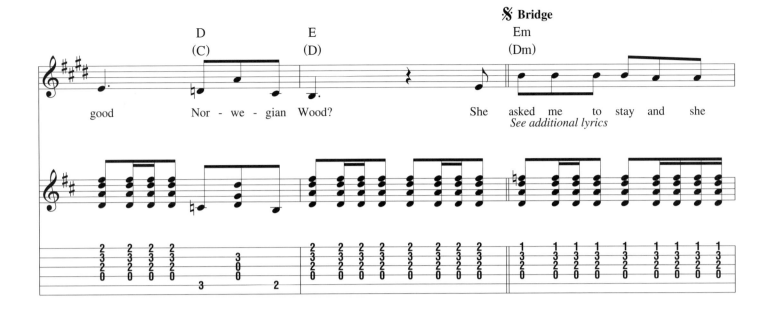

good Nor - we - gian Wood? She asked me to stay and she
See additional lyrics

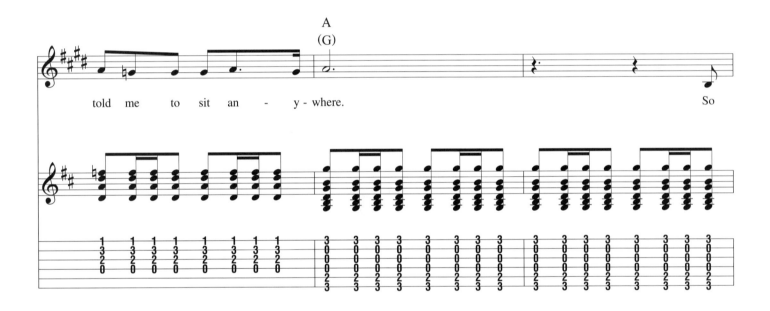

told me to sit an - y - where. So

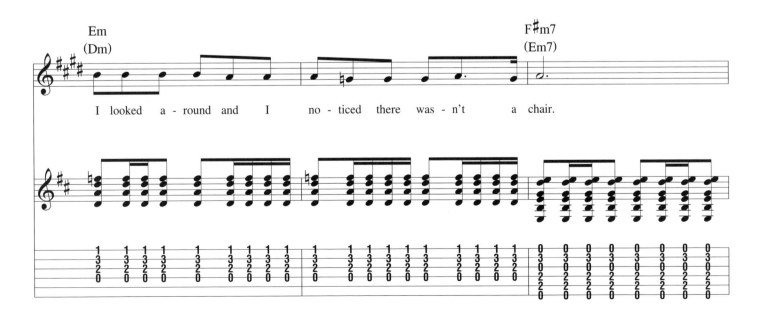

I looked a - round and I no - ticed there was - n't a chair.

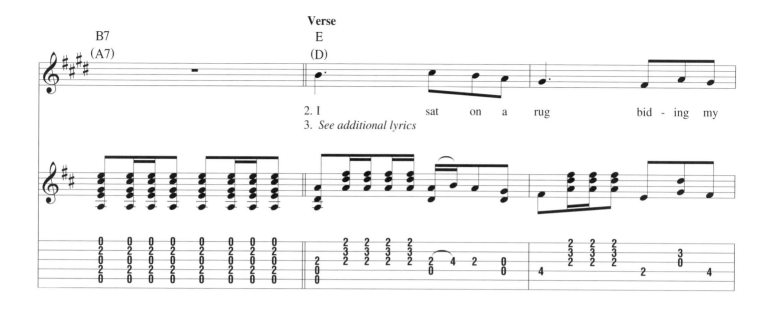

Verse

2. I   sat   on a rug   bid - ing my

3. *See additional lyrics*

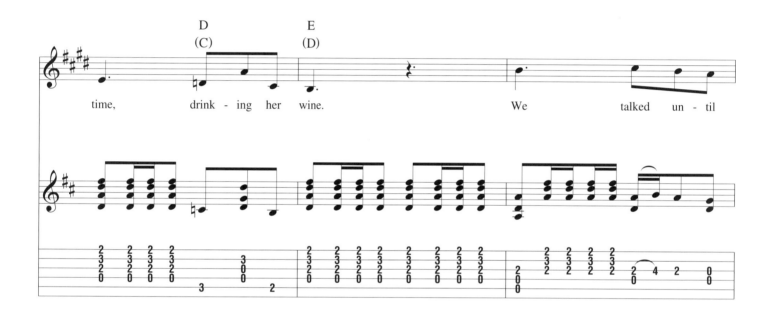

time,   drink - ing her wine.   We   talked un - til

To Coda ⊕

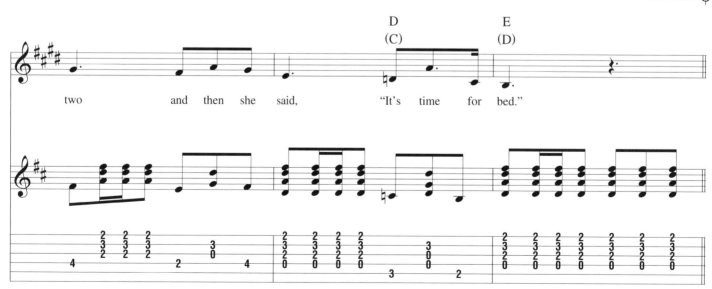

two   and then she said,   "It's time for bed."

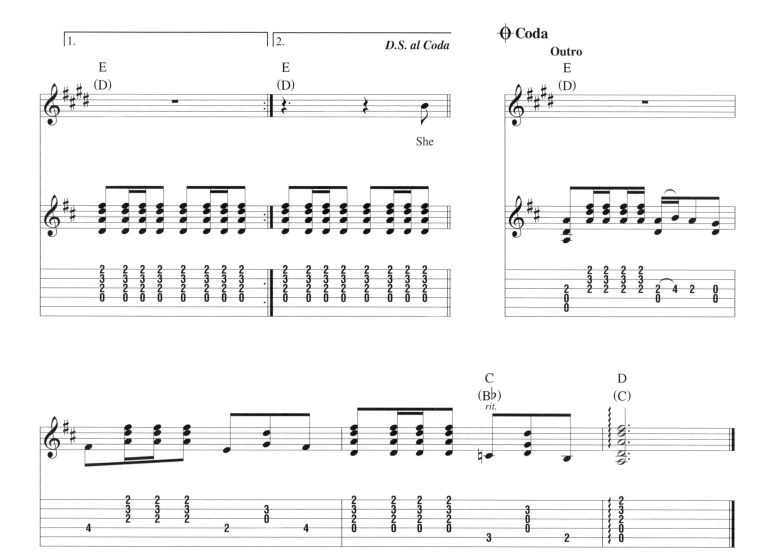

Additional Lyrics

Bridge She told me she worked in the morning and started to laugh.
I told her I didn't and crawled off to sleep in the bath.

3. And when I awoke I was alone; this bird had flown.
So, I lit a fire. Isn't it good Norwegian Wood?

3 AM

Lyrics by Rob Thomas
Music by Rob Thomas, Brian Yale, John Leslie Goff and John Joseph Stanley

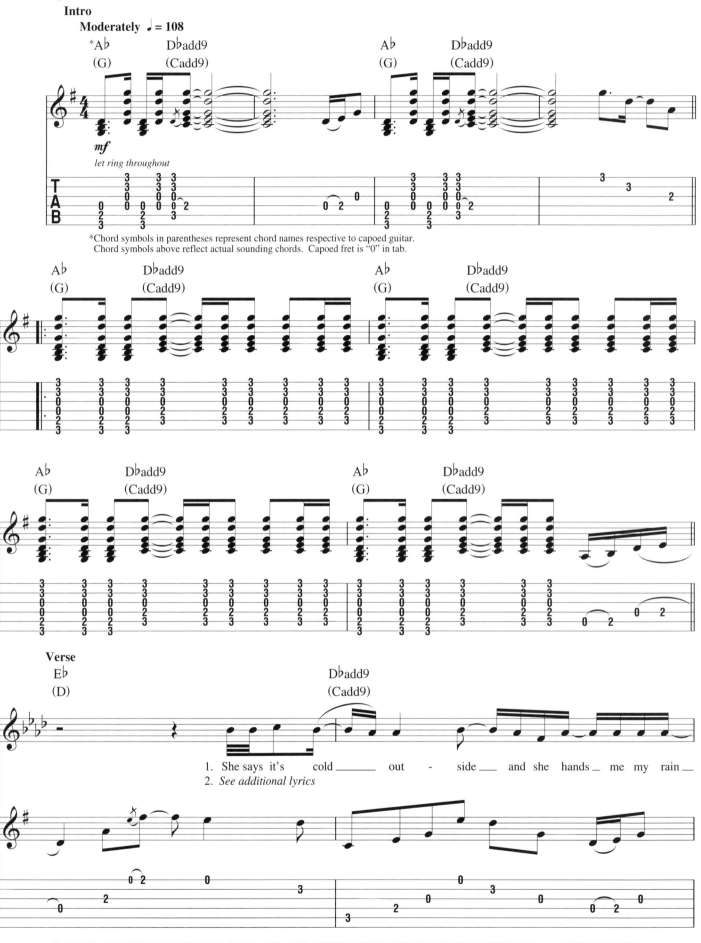

*Chord symbols in parentheses represent chord names respective to capoed guitar.
Chord symbols above reflect actual sounding chords. Capoed fret is "0" in tab.

1. She says it's cold _____ out - side ___ and she hands ___ me my rain ___
2. *See additional lyrics*

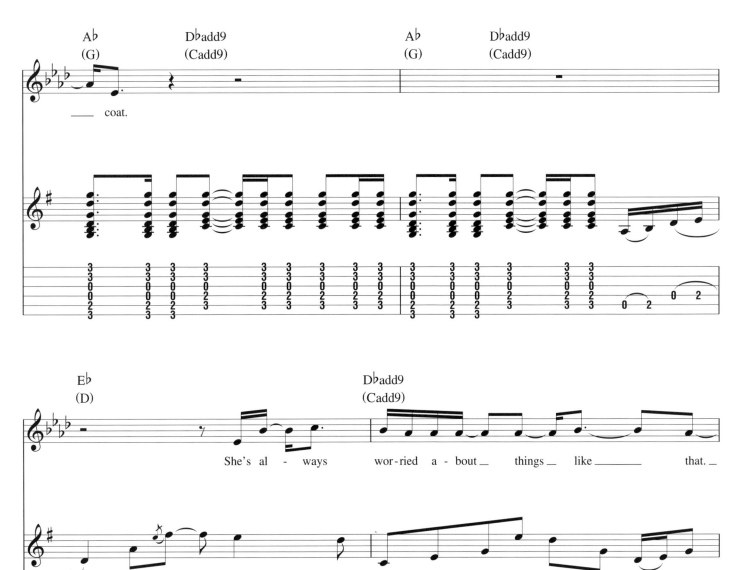

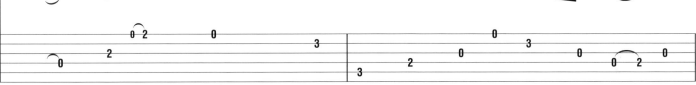

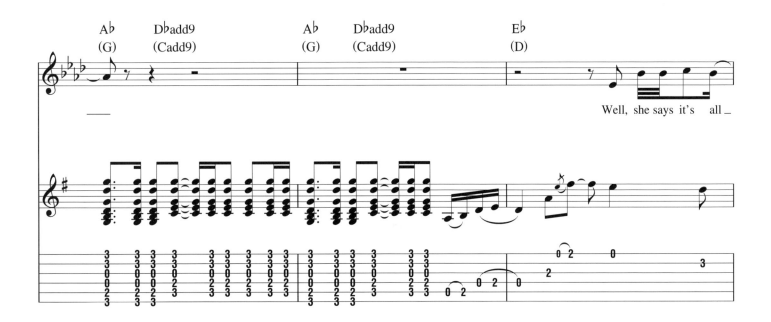

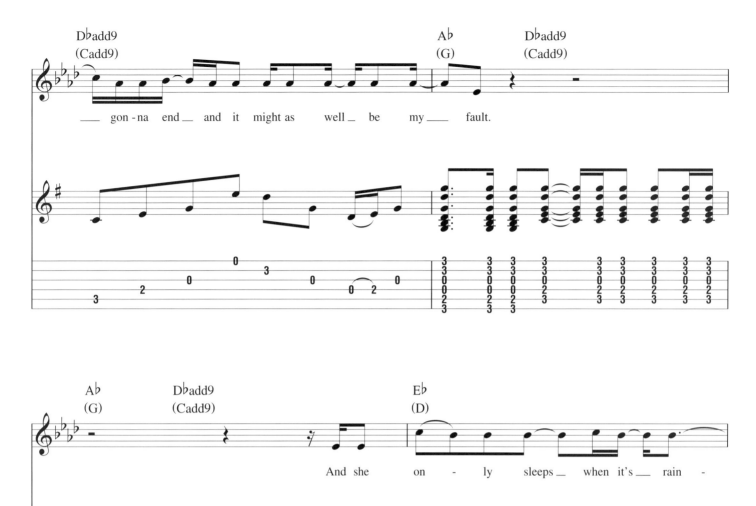

gon - na end _ and it might as well _ be my _ fault.

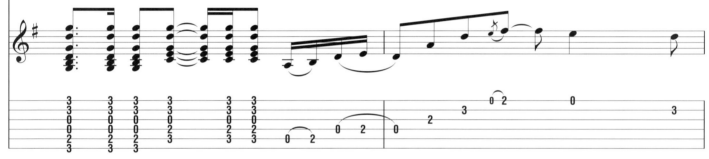

And she on - ly sleeps _ when it's _ rain -

- in'. And she screams, _____ and her voice _ is strain - in'. She says,

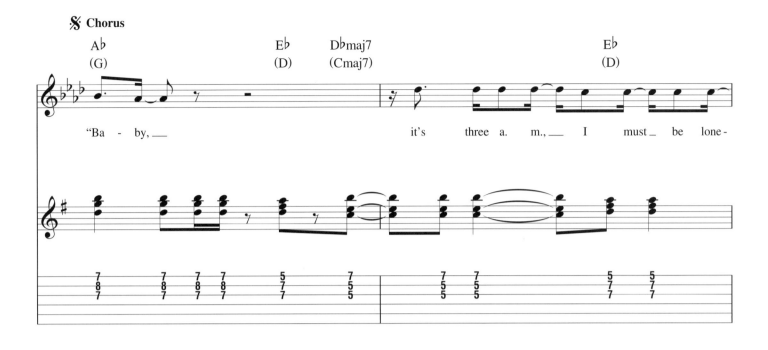

Chorus
A♭ (G) E♭ (D) D♭maj7 (Cmaj7) E♭ (D)
"Ba - by, it's three a. m., I must be lone - ly."
A♭ (G) E♭ (D) D♭maj7 (Cmaj7) E♭ (D) A♭ (G) E♭ (D) D♭maj7 (Cmaj7)
When she says, "Ba - by,
To Coda
E♭ (D) Fm (Em) E♭ (D) D♭add9 (Cadd9)
well, I can't help but be scared of it all some - times." And the

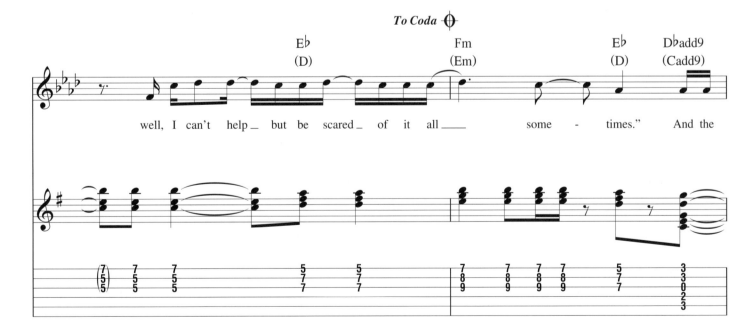

rain's gon-na wash a-way,_ I be-lieve it.   rain's gon-na wash a-way,_ I be-lieve,_

_ yes. _

Interlude

A♭   D♭add9   A♭   D♭add9
(G)   (Cadd9)   (G)   (Cadd9)

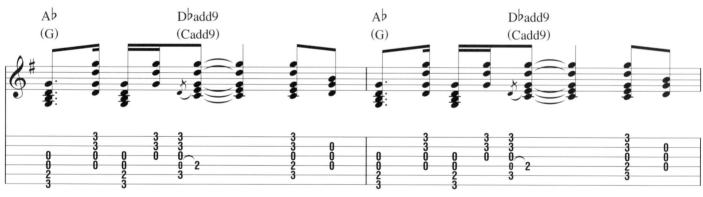

A♭   D♭add9   A♭   D♭add9
(G)   (Cadd9)   (G)   (Cadd9)

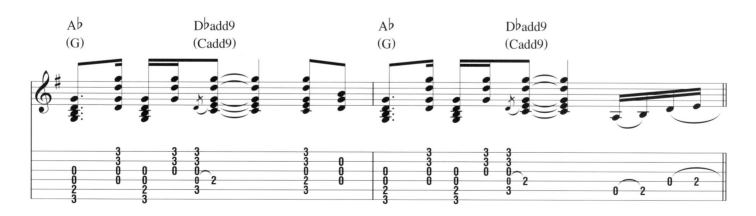

Verse

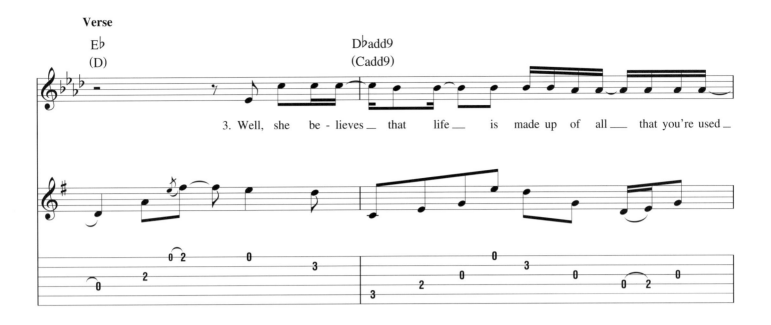

3. Well, she be-lieves __ that life __ is made up of all __ that you're used __

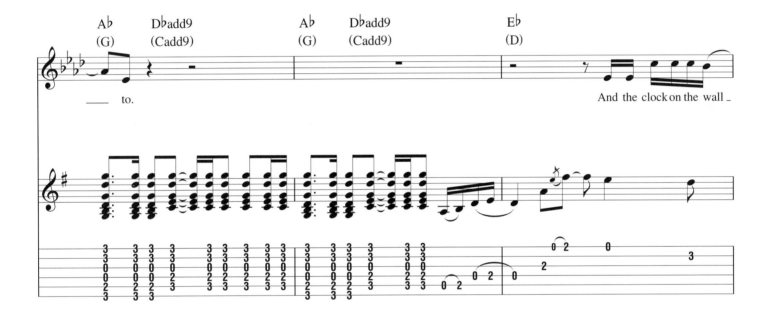

__ to.

And the clock on the wall __

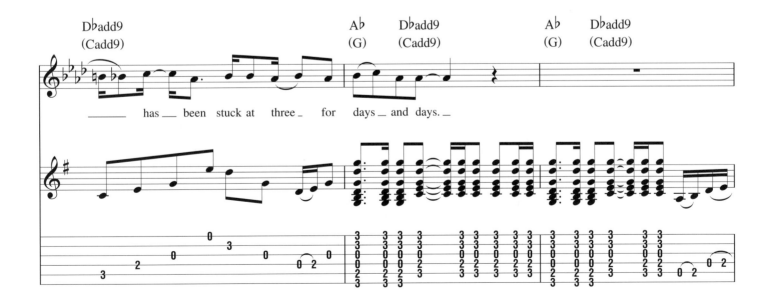

__ has __ been stuck at three __ for days __ and days. __

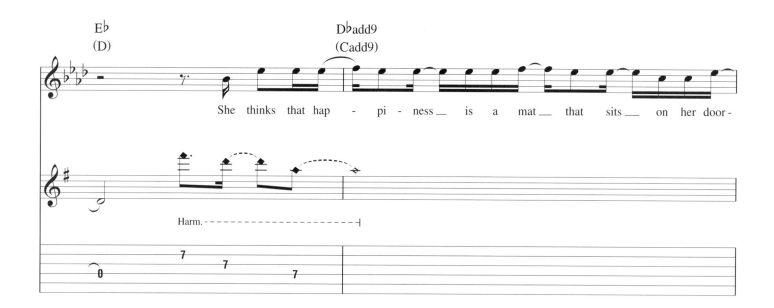

She thinks that hap - pi - ness_ is a mat_ that sits_ on her door-

- way,____ yeah. But out - side_ it stopped

D.S. al Coda

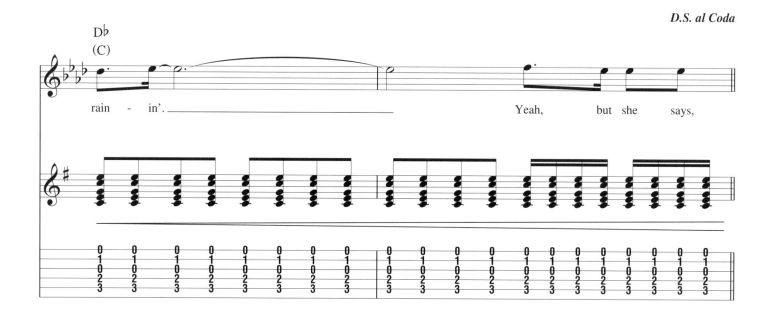

rain - in'._____ Yeah, but she says,

Coda

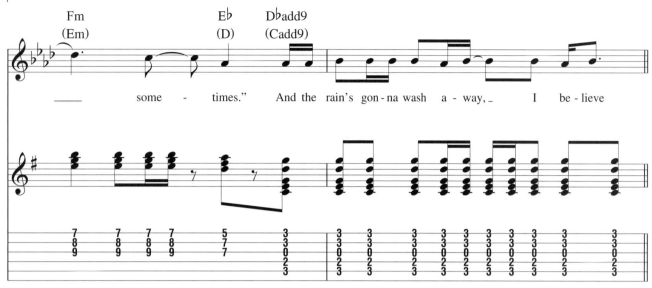

some - times." And the rain's gon-na wash a - way, __ I be - lieve

Outro

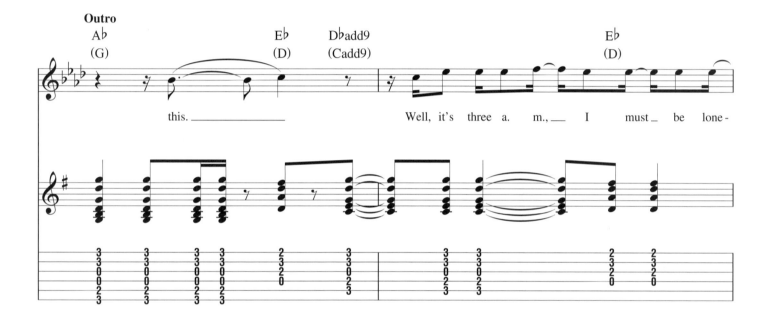

this. _____ Well, it's three a. m., __ I must __ be lone-

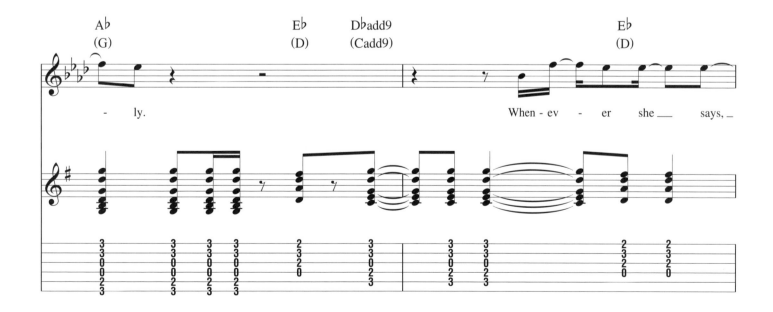

- ly. When - ev - er she __ says, __

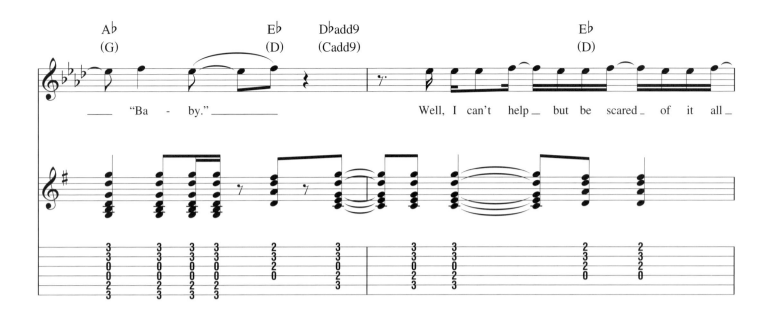

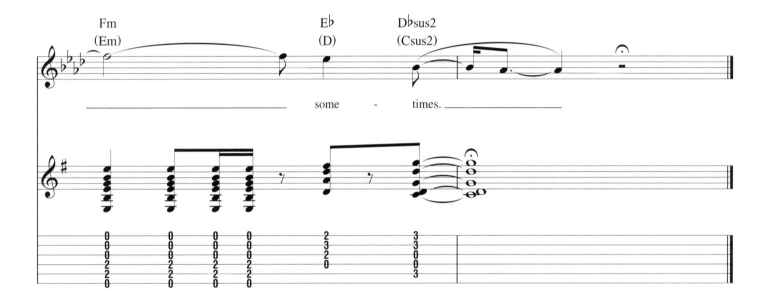

Additional Lyrics

2. But she's gotta little bit of somethin',
God, it's better than nothin'.
And in her color portrait world
She believes that she's got it all, all.
She swears the moon don't hang
Quite as high as it used to.
And she only sleeps when it's rainin'.
And she screams, and her voice is strainin'.

Guitar Notation Legend

THE MUSICAL STAFF shows pitches and rhythms and is divided by bar lines into measures. Pitches are named after the first seven letters of the alphabet.

TABLATURE graphically represents the guitar fingerboard. Each horizontal line represents a string, and each number represents a fret.

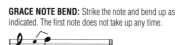

4th string, 2nd fret   1st & 2nd strings open, played together   open D chord

HALF-STEP BEND: Strike the note and bend up 1/2 step.

WHOLE-STEP BEND: Strike the note and bend up one step.

GRACE NOTE BEND: Strike the note and bend up as indicated. The first note does not take up any time.

SLIGHT (MICROTONE) BEND: Strike the note and bend up 1/4 step.

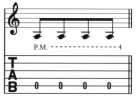

BEND AND RELEASE: Strike the note and bend up as indicated, then release back to the original note. Only the first note is struck.

PRE-BEND: Bend the note as indicated, then strike it.

VIBRATO: The string is vibrated by rapidly bending and releasing the note with the fretting hand.

PALM MUTING: The note is partially muted by the pick hand lightly touching the string(s) just before the bridge.

HAMMER-ON: Strike the first (lower) note with one finger, then sound the higher note (on the same string) with another finger by fretting it without picking.

PULL-OFF: Place both fingers on the notes to be sounded. Strike the first note and without picking, pull the finger off to sound the second (lower) note.

LEGATO SLIDE: Strike the first note and then slide the same fret-hand finger up or down to the second note. The second note is not struck.

SHIFT SLIDE: Same as legato slide, except the second note is struck.

TRILL: Very rapidly alternate between the notes indicated by continuously hammering on and pulling off.

TAPPING: Hammer ("tap") the fret indicated with the pick-hand index or middle finger and pull off to the note fretted by the fret hand.

NATURAL HARMONIC: Strike the note while the fret-hand lightly touches the string directly over the fret indicated.

PINCH HARMONIC: The note is fretted normally and a harmonic is produced by adding the edge of the thumb or the tip of the index finger of the pick hand to the normal pick attack.

TREMOLO PICKING: The note is picked as rapidly and continuously as possible.

VIBRATO BAR DIVE AND RETURN: The pitch of the note or chord is dropped a specified number of steps (in rhythm) then returned to the original pitch.

VIBRATO BAR SCOOP: Depress the bar just before striking the note, then quickly release the bar.

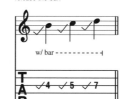

VIBRATO BAR DIP: Strike the note and then immediately drop a specified number of steps, then release back to the original pitch.

Additional Musical Definitions

(accent) • Accentuate note (play it louder)

(staccato) • Play the note short

D.S. al Coda • Go back to the sign (%), then play until the measure marked *"To Coda,"* then skip to the section labelled *"Coda."*

D.C. al Fine • Go back to the beginning of the song and play until the measure marked *"Fine"* (end).

Fill • Label used to identify a brief melodic figure which is to be inserted into the arrangement.

N.C. • Instrument is silent (drops out).

• Repeat measures between signs.

1. 2. • When a repeated section has different endings, play the first ending only the first time and the second ending only the second time.

HAL•LEONARD GUITAR PLAY•ALONG

This series will help you play your favorite songs quickly and easily. Just follow the tab and listen to the CD to hear how the guitar should sound, and then play along using the separate backing tracks. Mac or PC users can also slow down the tempo without changing pitch by using the CD in their computer. The melody and lyrics are included in the book so that you can sing or simply follow along.

INCLUDES TAB

VOL. 1 – ROCK GUITAR 00699570 / $14.95
Day Tripper • Message in a Bottle • Refugee • Shattered • Sunshine of Your Love • Takin' Care of Business • Tush • Walk This Way.

VOL. 2 – ACOUSTIC 00699569 / $14.95
Angie • Behind Blue Eyes • Best of My Love • Blackbird • Dust in the Wind • Layla • Night Moves • Yesterday.

VOL. 3 – HARD ROCK 00699573 / $14.95
Crazy Train • Iron Man • Living After Midnight • Rock You like a Hurricane • Round and Round • Smoke on the Water • Sweet Child O' Mine • You Really Got Me.

VOL. 4 – POP/ROCK 00699571 / $14.95
Breakdown • Crazy Little Thing Called Love • Hit Me with Your Best Shot • I Want You to Want Me • Lights • R.O.C.K. in the U.S.A. • Summer of '69 • What I Like About You.

VOL. 5 – MODERN ROCK 00699574 / $14.95
Aerials • Alive • Bother • Chop Suey! • Control • Last Resort • Take a Look Around (Theme from *M:I-2*) • Wish You Were Here.

VOL. 6 – '90S ROCK 00699572 / $14.95
Are You Gonna Go My Way • Come Out and Play • I'll Stick Around • Know Your Enemy • Man in the Box • Outshined • Smells Like Teen Spirit • Under the Bridge.

VOL. 7 – BLUES GUITAR 00699575 / $14.95
All Your Love (I Miss Loving) • Born Under a Bad Sign • Hide Away • I'm Tore Down • I'm Your Hoochie Coochie Man • Pride and Joy • Sweet Home Chicago • The Thrill Is Gone.

VOL. 8 – ROCK 00699585 / $14.95
All Right Now • Black Magic Woman • Get Back • Hey Joe • Layla • Love Me Two Times • Won't Get Fooled Again • You Really Got Me.

VOL. 9 – PUNK ROCK 00699576 / $14.95
All the Small Things • Fat Lip • Flavor of the Weak • I Feel So • Lifestyles of the Rich and Famous• Say It Ain't So • Self Esteem (So) Tired of Waiting for You.

VOL. 10 – ACOUSTIC 00699586 / $14.95
Here Comes the Sun • Landslide • The Magic Bus • Norwegian Wood (This Bird Has Flown) • Pink Houses • Space Oddity • Tangled Up in Blue • Tears in Heaven.

VOL. 11 – EARLY ROCK 00699579 / $14.95
Fun, Fun, Fun • Hound Dog • Louie, Louie • No Particular Place to Go • Oh, Pretty Woman • Rock Around the Clock • Under the Boardwalk • Wild Thing.

VOL. 12 – POP/ROCK 00699587 / $14.95
867-5309/Jenny • Every Breath You Take • Money for Nothing • Rebel, Rebel • Run to You • Ticket to Ride • Wonderful Tonight • You Give Love a Bad Name.

VOL. 13 – FOLK ROCK 00699581 / $14.95
Annie's Song • Leaving on a Jet Plane • Suite: Judy Blue Eyes • This Land Is Your Land • Time in a Bottle • Turn! Turn! Turn! • You've Got a Friend • You've Got to Hide Your Love Away.

VOL. 14 – BLUES ROCK 00699582 / $14.95
Blue on Black • Crossfire • Cross Road Blues (Crossroads) • The House Is Rockin' • La Grange • Move It on Over • Roadhouse Blues • Statesboro Blues.

VOL. 15 – R&B 00699583 / $14.95
Ain't Too Proud to Beg • Brick House • Get Ready • I Can't Help Myself • I Got You (I Feel Good) • I Heard It Through the Grapevine • My Girl • Shining Star.

VOL. 16 – JAZZ 00699584 / $14.95
All Blues • Bluesette • Footprints • How Insensitive • Misty • Satin Doll • Stella by Starlight • Tenor Madness.

VOL. 17 – COUNTRY 00699588 / $14.95
Amie • Boot Scootin' Boogie • Chattahoochee • Folsom Prison Blues • Friends in Low Places • Forever and Ever, Amen • T-R-O-U-B-L-E • Workin' Man Blues.

VOL. 18 – ACOUSTIC ROCK 00699577 / $14.95
About a Girl • Breaking the Girl • Drive • Iris • More Than Words • Patience • Silent Lucidity • 3 AM.

VOL. 19 – SOUL 00699578 / $14.95
Get Up (I Feel Like Being) a Sex Machine • Green Onions • In the Midnight Hour • Knock on Wood • Mustang Sally • Respect • (Sittin' On) the Dock of the Bay • Soul Man.

VOL. 20 – ROCKABILLY 00699580 / $14.95
Be-Bop-A-Lula • Blue Suede Shoes • Hello Mary Lou • Little Sister • Mystery Train • Rock This Town • Stray Cat Strut • That'll Be the Day.

VOL. 21 – YULETIDE 00699602 / $14.95
Angels We Have Heard on High • Away in a Manger • Deck the Hall • The First Noel • Go, Tell It on the Mountain • Jingle Bells • Joy to the World • O Little Town of Bethlehem.

VOL. 22 – CHRISTMAS 00699600 / $14.95
The Christmas Song • Frosty the Snow Man • Happy Xmas • Here Comes Santa Claus • Jingle-Bell Rock • Merry Christmas, Darling • Rudolph the Red-Nosed Reindeer • Silver Bells.

VOL. 23 – SURF 00699635 / $14.95
Let's Go Trippin' • Out of Limits • Penetration • Pipeline • Surf City • Surfin' U.S.A. • Walk Don't Run • The Wedge.

VOL. 24 – ERIC CLAPTON 00699649 / $14.95
Badge • Bell Bottom Blues • Change the World • Cocaine • Key to the Highway • Lay Down Sally • White Room • Wonderful Tonight.

VOL. 25 – LENNON & McCARTNEY 00699642 / $14.95
Back in the U.S.S.R. • Drive My Car • Get Back • A Hard Day's Night • I Feel Fine • Paperback Writer • Revolution • Ticket to Ride.

VOL. 26 – ELVIS PRESLEY 00699643 / $14.95
All Shook Up • Blue Suede Shoes • Don't Be Cruel • Heartbreak Hotel • Hound Dog • Jailhouse Rock • Little Sister • Mystery Train.

VOL. 27 – DAVID LEE ROTH 00699645 / $14.95
Ain't Talkin' 'Bout Love • Dance the Night Away • Hot for Teacher • Just Like Paradise • A Lil' Ain't Enough • Runnin' with the Devil • Unchained • Yankee Rose.

VOL. 28 – GREG KOCH 00699646 / $14.95
Chief's Blues • Death of a Bassman • Dylan the Villain • The Grip • Holy Grail • Spank It • Tonus Diabolicus • Zoiks.

VOL. 29 – BOB SEGER 00699647 / $14.95
Against the Wind • Betty Lou's Gettin' Out Tonight • Hollywood Nights • Mainstreet • Night Moves • Old Time Rock & Roll • Rock and Roll Never Forgets • Still the Same.

VOL. 30 – KISS 00699644 / $14.95
Cold Gin • Detroit Rock City • Deuce • Firehouse • Heaven's on Fire • Love Gun • Rock and Roll All Nite • Shock Me.

VOL. 31 – CHRISTMAS HITS 00699652 / $14.95
Blue Christmas • Do You Hear What I Hear • Happy Holiday • I Saw Mommy Kissing Santa Claus • I'll Be Home for Christmas • Let It Snow! Let It Snow! Let It Snow! • Little Saint Nick • Snowfall.

VOL. 32 – THE OFFSPRING 00699653 / $14.95
Bad Habit • Come Out and Play • Gone Away • Gotta Get Away • Hit That • The Kids Aren't Alright • Pretty Fly (For a White Guy) • Self Esteem.

VOL. 33 – ACOUSTIC CLASSICS 00699656 / $14.95
Across the Universe • Babe, I'm Gonna Leave You • Crazy on You • Heart of Gold • Hotel California • I'd Love to Change the World • Thick As a Brick • Wanted Dead or Alive.

VOL. 34 – CLASSIC ROCK 00699658 / $14.95
Aqualung • Born to Be Wild • The Boys Are Back in Town • Brown Eyed Girl • Reeling in the Years • Rock'n Me • Rocky Mountain Way • Sweet Emotion.

VOL. 35 – HAIR METAL 00699660 / $14.95
Decadence Dance • Don't Treat Me Bad • Down Boys • Seventeen • Shake Me • Up All Night • Wait • Talk Dirty to Me.

VOL. 36 – SOUTHERN ROCK 00699661 / $14.95
Can't You See • Flirtin' with Disaster • Hold on Loosely • Jessica • Mississippi Queen • Ramblin' Man • Sweet Home Alabama • What's Your Name.

VOL. 37 – ACOUSTIC METAL 00699662 / $14.95
Every Rose Has Its Thorn • Fly to the Angels • Hole Hearted • Love Is on the Way • Love of a Lifetime • Signs • To Be with You • When the Children Cry.

VOL. 38 – BLUES 00699663 / $14.95
Boom Boom • Cold Shot • Crosscut Saw • Everyday I Have the Blues • Frosty • Further On up the Road • Killing Floor • Texas Flood.

VOL. 39 – '80S METAL 00699664 / $14.95
Bark at the Moon • Big City Nights • Breaking the Chains • Cult of Personality • Lay It Down • Living on a Prayer • Panama • Smokin' in the Boys Room.

VOL. 40 – INCUBUS 00699668 / $14.95
Are You In? • Drive • Megalomaniac • Nice to Know You • Pardon Me • Stellar • Talk Shows on Mute • Wish You Were Here.

VOL. 41 – ERIC CLAPTON 00699669 / $14.95
After Midnight • Can't Find My Way Home • Forever Man • I Shot the Sheriff • I'm Tore Down • Pretending • Running on Faith • Tears in Heaven.

VOL. 42 – CHART HITS 00699670 / $14.95
Are You Gonna Be My Girl • Heaven • Here Without You • I Believe in a Thing Called Love • Just Like You • Last Train Home • This Love • Until the Day I Die.

VOL. 43 – LYNYRD SKYNYRD 00699681 / $14.95
Don't Ask Me No Questions • Free Bird • Gimme Three Steps • I Know a Little • Saturday Night Special • Sweet Home Alabama • That Smell • You Got That Right.

VOL. 44 – JAZZ 00699689 / $14.95
I Remember You • I'll Remember April • Impressions • In a Mellow Tone • Moonlight in Vermont • On a Slow Boat to China • Things Ain't What They Used to Be • Yesterdays.

VOL. 46 – MAINSTREAM ROCK 00699722 / $14.95
Just a Girl • Keep Away • Kryptonite • Lightning Crashes • 1979 • One Step Closer • Scar Tissue • Torn.

VOL. 47 – HENDRIX SMASH HITS 00699723/ $16.95
All Along the Watchtower • Can You See Me? • Crosstown Traffic • Fire • Foxey Lady • Hey Joe • Manic Depression • Purple Haze • Red House • Remember • Stone Free • The Wind Cries Mary.

VOL. 48 – AEROSMITH CLASSICS 00699724 / $14.95
Back in the Saddle • Draw the Line • Dream On • Last Child • Mama Kin • Same Old Song & Dance • Sweet Emotion • Walk This Way.

VOL. 50 – NÜ METAL 00699726 / $14.95
Duality • Here to Stay • In the End • Judith • Nookie • So Cold • Toxicity • Whatever.

VOL. 51 – ALTERNATIVE '90S 00699727 / $14.95
Alive • Cherub Rock • Come As You Are • Give It Away • Jane Says • No Excuses • No Rain • Santeria.

VOL. 56 – FOO FIGHTERS 00699749 / $14.95
All My Life • Best of You • DOA • I'll Stick Around • Learn to Fly • Monkey Wrench • My Hero • This Is a Call.

VOL. 57 – SYSTEM OF A DOWN 00699751 / $14.95
Aerials • B.Y.O.B. • Chop Suey! • Innervision • Question! • Spiders • Sugar • Toxicity.

Prices, contents, and availability subject to change without notice.

FOR MORE INFORMATION, SEE YOUR LOCAL MUSIC DEALER, OR WRITE TO:

7777 W. BLUEMOUND RD. P.O. BOX 13819 MILWAUKEE, WI 53213

Visit Hal Leonard online at www.halleonard.com

0106